Singing Meadow

*The Adventure of
Creating a Country Home*

Rejoice in wildness!
Warm good wishes to
Leona
Peri

Singing Meadow

The Adventure of
Creating a Country Home

by

Peri McQuay

If you have built castles in the air, your work need not be lost;
that is where they should be. Now put the foundations under them.
Henry David Thoreau

WINTERGREEN
STUDIOS PRESS

Wintergreen Studios Press
Township of South Frontenac
PO Box 75, Yarker, ON, Canada K0K 3N0

Wintergreen Studios Press (WSP) gratefully acknowledges the financial support received from Wintergreen Studios.

Every effort has been made to contact the copyright holders, artists, photographers, and authors whose work appears in this text for permission to reprint material. We regret any oversights and we will be happy to rectify them in future editions.

Book and cover design by Rena Upitis
Edited by Sara L. Beck
Front cover painting: Peri's childhood home, painted by her artist father, Ken Phillips
Back cover photo by Rena Upitis
Composed in Book Antiqua and Candara, typefaces designed by Monotype Typography and Gary Munch, respectively.

Library and Archives Canada Cataloguing in Publication

McQuay, Peri Phillips. 1945 –

Singing Meadow: The Adventure of Creating a Country Home/Peri McQuay

ISBN: 978-0-9918722-3-7

1. House and Home – General.
2. Nature – Environmental Conservation & Protection.
3. Design – General.
I. Title. Singing Meadow: The Adventure of Creating a Country Home.

Legal Deposit – Library and Archives Canada

Other Books by Peri Phillips McQuay

The View from Foley Mountain.
Toronto, ON: Natural Heritage, 1995.

A Wing in the Door: Life with a Red-tailed Hawk.
Minneapolis, MN: Milkweed Editions, 2001.

For all those who dream of a small house in the country and to Barry, my beloved husband, who has inspired me and travelled with me on our long journey together.

Contents

Introduction xi

Searching 1

Falling in Love 22

Time of Waiting 35

Planning in Earnest 47

Breaking the Soil 91

Moving Ahead 97

Underway at Last 109

Coming Along Quickly 149

The Last Big Push 158

Harvest 171

Leaving Day 175

Circling Home 177

Barry 183

Afterword 185

Acknowledgements 187

Bibliography 189

Introduction

I didn't think there was anywhere like that left now.

My heart leaps. It is twilight, and I am turning off the crowded highway, headed north. In the opposite lane I am aware of a string of slow-moving cars travelling back to the city. These are the cars of people returning from brief country weekends. But for me, the beautiful northland, abundant with lakes, forests, fields and hills, is no mere holiday retreat. Circling and climbing on "the long and winding road", I am headed home. Knowing that this is my native land makes my heart soar with gladness.

Some years before, my husband and I were seated in the office of a Toronto funeral director while Barry signed the final documents following my mother-in-law's burial. "Westport?" the middle-aged director asked casually, reading from his copy of the forms. "Where's that?" Although we were numbed by the preceding painful days, we politely sketched in a few details. Our home, we told him, was in the middle of eight hundred reasonably wild acres of a conservation area overlooking a little village of seven hundred people and six churches on the shores of the beautiful Little Rideau Lake. Barry was supervisor of the park, and living on-site was part of his job. What he most loved about working there was teaching children and public of all ages about nature.

With the director now leaning forward in his seat, we expanded. Our village was a friendly place where running errands could be a slow process as we stopped all along the street to talk with many friends. Our two sons had gone to the little school across the lake. This rural community was a place where children still could safely roam free, sure in the knowledge that many villagers were watching out for them. Indeed, this was the kind of place where neighbours still cared, bringing food and helping out if someone was sick or in trouble. "They do?" blurted the funeral director, leaning across his desk. A minute later, he said thoughtfully, "I didn't think there was anywhere like that left now."

Encouraged by the director's interest, we were tempted to add a bit more. Deer and many other creatures often walked right by our house in the park, we told him. Standing on our back porch at night, listening to the coyotes sing to the stars, we could not see another light. Our home was a place where we enjoyed being fairly self-sufficient, with a large vegetable garden that supplied our needs throughout most of the year.

As we handed the signed papers back to our listener and stood to leave, he exclaimed, "I wish I could live in a place like that. That would be my dream." Recalling the miles of drab, treeless suburbs we had passed en route to our meeting with him, we understood his longing. In North America, the luxury of a country home is becoming a rarity now. For us, it's a privilege we never take for granted.

For thirty years, we lived at the Foley Mountain Conservation Area, moving as freely and joyously as the resident park deer herd, scrambling over granite ridges, hearing the swelling wind in the pines, sitting watching the ice form on remote ponds. While there, we raised our two sons, Morgan and Jeremy, teaching them to love nature as we did, and Barry and I were lucky enough to discover our true vocations. Barry was passionately committed to teaching environmental education to thousands of school children. Rejoicing in living closely with the rocks, ponds, abandoned fields, and forests of the area, I found that I, too, was eager to share what I was discovering and began the writing that eventually led to my nature books, *The View From Foley Mountain* and *A Wing in the Door*.

It was a rich life, full of delight in our surroundings close to the land, and blessed with many friendships. But in time, change made living within a park less desirable for us. Sometimes, when there was talk of harvesting the beloved pines and shag-bark hickories to turn profit for the hard-pressed conservation authority, I could only wish I owned this land and could prevent ravages to it. After the election of Mike Harris's neo-conservative provincial government, fund-raising consumed increasingly large amounts of the time Barry used to spend caring for the park and sharing its lessons with visitors. He saw poor people turn away from their park as he administered the new gate fees that put an end to equal access for all; he saw that children from the more impoverished areas no longer were able to take advantage of his education programs because fees had been imposed, while ones from more affluent schools came less often. Inevitably, staff meetings became simply times to wrangle about money rather than a sharing of ideas about how to make services work more effectively. "I'm a teacher, not a fundraiser," he stormed. "Wrapping coins and coming up with new ways to tease a few dollars out of people is not how I want to spend my life."

Over the years, with the help of the warm-hearted community nestled below "the mountain," we had achieved what we wanted — assurance that this beautiful park would continue to be cherished and that the environmental education programs that Barry had developed would continue. Ironically though, this very success made Foley Mountain less of a home for me.

For a writer, living in an office-home where the phone rang frequently and people dropped in any time of day or night was difficult. Solitude and reflective time are essential for me. It was painful to abandon my train of thought to talk with the increasing numbers of visitors who now walked the trails and who stopped by our house frequently. As the town and the park became busier, there was rarely a time of quiet to walk the trail overlooking the lake. Even in winter when I went out before dawn to listen for owls, my hearing sometimes was dimmed by the grinding gears of heavy trucks ascending the big hill just west of the park. I longed to create a sense of sanctuary for myself.

Living in the old rented farmhouse within the park was both a requirement and a benefit of the job. Once, we had wished for nothing more than to live in the park forever. Now, as Barry's retirement approached, we accepted that the residence would be needed for another supervisor, but we also recognized that it was time for us to leave. The trouble was that this meant we would need to find another place to live.

For the first time in our lives, we would be in a position to own a home. In my mind I was starting to think about what the idea of home meant to me. As I began to shape plans for a much longed for country place of my own, in my mind I was calling it *Heart's Desire*.

I

Searching

Before we knew it, after so many years of waiting and dreaming and fearing, the time for us to begin searching for a new home approached. In just a couple more years we would experience not only the wrench of leaving the park, but also the adventure of moving to a new life.

But where would we go? Always we had lived in rented homes, walked rented land. Because of this, whenever we were away from home we played the game of looking for somewhere permanent to live. "That one," Barry would say, pointing across the road. "It's the upstairs bay window. That reminds me of my grandparents' house."

"What about this?" I would ask another time, craning my head out the car window to study a small stone cottage beside a tumbling brook and set back from the road. There scarcely was a drive when we didn't find somewhere we thought we might like to live. Now, though, after thirty years of dreaming of a house of our own, the search would become a reality.

Perhaps because we had waited so long and had rehearsed so often, we believed we knew exactly what we wanted. First on our list was land of our own, or somewhere we could walk. Loving the wild fields and forests at Foley Mountain had confirmed this for us. There would be fifty to a hundred acres, we decided, with beaver ponds, marshes and hills, as well as alluring fields enclosed by trees, which led from one to the other like rooms. The place would be a haven for birds, surprising us with new species and delighting us with old acquaintances. Most importantly, we needed to have a variety of significant trees — beech, maple, oak, white pine, yellow and white birches, shagbark hickories. I hoped to spend my later years listening to the wind in the trees as I had in the encircling forest of my childhood. If there were some established gardens too, well, that would be wonderful.

In our minds' eyes, our new home was vividly real. In fact, it surely was waiting for us to find it. We would go down a long, winding, wooded laneway to a clearing and there it would be: a welcoming, sheltering old farmhouse with a large nearby tree or two for shade. When we entered this house, there would be that sigh of thankfulness. "Home at last." As well as being a farmhouse, we expected this new home would be light and airy. Of course it would have a big kitchen where people could gather to keep me company while I cooked, or perhaps an open-concept living room, dining room and kitchen combined. And some well-defined separate spaces for Barry and me would probably be a good idea. Some surprising, sheltered nooks, was what we said to ourselves. And, oh yes, windows, above all else, windows. After nearly thirty years of living in a 1920s farmhouse with small, narrow windows, we hungered to watch sunrise and sunset.

But whenever my imagination became too high-flown, the thought of nature writer Helen Hoover brought me back to what mattered most. Years ago, when I was only dreaming of living close to wildness, I came upon her *A Place in the Woods*, and reading this inspiring memoir made all the difference in my life. Helen, an award-winning metallurgist, and her art director husband, Adrian, were living at a hectic pace in Chicago. But then, on their first trip to the Lake Superior shore, they bought a log cabin as a vacation spot. Before long, there came a time when the Hoovers found they couldn't bear to leave this primitive rustic home and return to the city.

How much would you sacrifice for a dream as important as living surrounded by nature? Just six weeks after their stay became permanent, Helen and Ade lost their car in a collision on a narrow, snow-covered road. That accident not only left them without transportation, but also prevented Ade's getting to Duluth to sign a contract for artwork. Now the middle-aged pair were left almost broke and with no conceivable future income. Simply fetching the mail was a wearying six-mile excursion. They could only order groceries rarely, and when they did order them, they had to be fetched by boat or, in winter, hauled in packsacks. Although Hoover was candid about the many hardships they experienced, including worrying accidents and a fire, what resonated for me about her story was her passionate commitment to her rugged land.

Hoover's moving narrative of life in the north woods inspired Barry and me to leave the relative security and comfortable pay of Barry's high school teaching job in 1975 for our own more difficult and uncertain life on Foley Mountain's eight hundred acres. From that time on, in our own way, we were hoping to live closer to nature and to become constant observers.

Often, too, I remembered the ideal of economist E.F. Schumacher: "the maximum well-being with the minimum consumption." It was then that I learned to ask the hard questions: "How much do you want this dream of living closely with land?" "How much do you need?" Throughout our search, and in spite of many temptations away from simple living, these were ideals that would keep us true.

But where would we go? We all have a zone that feels native to us, a circle of reference. In theory, once Barry was retired we could choose to live anywhere. Proximity to a town would not matter since we would not be dependent on a job location, and we were relatively able. But how big an area should we consider? After much thought, we set our limits to include much of eastern Ontario. Many who had retired recommended that we should move away from Westport once Barry was done. We imagined making new friends and connecting with new services in the easy way we used to do many years ago before we moved to the park.

Over the long winter, occasionally I went shopping for presents for the house we did not yet have. In the back of my mind lurked the irrational notion that doing so just might bring the house closer. In antique stores, I mooned over small treasures, feeling a tenderness towards this unknown house. I even considered bringing home an antique door for it, or a small stained glass window light to place over the door, where it would capture sun to cast beams of coloured light into the hall. Our best find, though, came when Barry and I were exploring a large Quebec emporium. Opening his hand to show me an enchanting acorn and oak leaf door knocker, Barry asked, "What about this?" Of course we bought it. We couldn't help ourselves. We explained sheepishly to the sales clerk that we didn't have the house yet, but that maybe this would help us find the right place. From then on, at low moments we would unwrap the door knocker, fondling it as if it might indeed show us the way.

As we prepared, I imagined that our search would be an interesting journey. "At the very least, it will be fun seeing inside other people's houses," I told Barry, who was not looking forward to the process. "You forget," he said glumly, "I hate change. I just want to stay where we are." And in fact, if that had been possible we would happily have lived at Foley Mountain for the rest of our days. However, as we set out to find a suitable house, neither of us knew how profoundly our quest for a new home would change our lives and our view of what was possible.

At first we dabbled, testing the water. "Original, fourth generation farmhouse on Amherst Island," Barry read to me one autumn Saturday while we were dawdling over breakfast. "That sounds interesting." We knew it was time to make a start, and Amherst Island, on Lake Ontario, was one of our special places, still largely unspoiled, with rolling farms stretching to the shores, forests, and even a famous owl woods. Naturalists come to this precious island to view the many migrant birds who rest there before or after crossing the broad lake. "We'll make a day of it," we told ourselves. "After we've looked at the property we can drive around a bit."

Standing by the rail of the Amherst Island ferry, listening as the engine roared into reverse, labouring against a stiff wind to line up with the dock, I muttered to Barry, "We really don't know what we're doing. We don't have any idea what to ask the real estate agent."

"This is just practice," he reminded me, as we hurried back to climb into our car. "It's not very likely we are going to want the first house we find." All the same, in spite of the chilly, slatey grey day, we felt good the minute we drove off the ferry, sheltered in an island world set apart. Jane, the brisk, friendly real estate agent, stepped across the little car park to meet us, red coat flying, and invited us into her station wagon. As she drove, she gestured lavishly at favourite buildings along the way, giving us a sense of a close, caring community. "Do either of you sing?" she asked hopefully. "That is our church, over there on the left. We have a nice little choir, but we're always looking for new members."

Soon after, she pulled into a long maple-lined laneway. "Here we are." We studied the white, gabled farmhouse with big snowball bushes up against the house. Beyond it there was even a barn. "We go around the back, of course," the agent said as she hurried us along through the light drizzle that was beginning to fall. "It's kind of sad, really. Horace has lived here all of his life: eighty-six years, that is. He did fine until his wife May died five years ago. Even after that, he hung on here, actually made a few improvements, which you'll see when we go in." She was remembering her job as agent, now, drawing back from her natural friendliness in the car. A tired-looking, middle-aged daughter opened the door to us and invited us into an immense farm kitchen. In a corner by a long window, sat the father, wrapped in a plaid brown rug, clutching the arms of his chair. While we looked around, feeling like the intruders that we were, Jane chatted naturally with Cindy, the daughter. I hadn't liked to look over at the father, but when I did, he gave me a sweet, forlorn smile. "A lot of happy times, here," he said. "*I* think I could stay on. It just doesn't seem right. And what will I take with me? How could I possibly know what I would need?" Seeing his misery my heart shrank.

Jane stepped in quickly, "Come in, I'll show you around. This, as you see, is the kitchen. A lot of great get-togethers here, haven't there been, Horace?" she said, without giving the old man a chance to answer. I was familiar with farmhouse kitchens, and most often I liked them. Once I had enjoyed living with one where we had room for a full-sized chest freezer, and where, on rainy days, Barry and our three-year-old son Morgan sometimes played soccer while I made my bread. Glancing quickly around this one, though, I was dismayed with the few, homemade cabinets, in some dark wood substitute. For the first time we heard an agent say, "There's a lot of potential here."

"The wiring?" I asked, looking at a very old extension cord stretched across the end of the room. "It would need to be upgraded, of course, as you would expect with an older home," Jane answered briskly, leading us past a broad, but gloomy, hall with coat hooks, and no closet, and up a finely made staircase.

"Don't look at the family photos, the puzzles lying spilled on the floor, the headless teddy bear, the framed religious mottos," I told myself. "Try to envision your own things—the loom, for instance, where would that go?" But in all the houses we were to see, I never completely acquired the necessary knack of ignoring. I couldn't envision ugly wallpaper gone, heavy, closed curtains removed.

"Come on, Peri, let's just get going," urged Barry, pulling me aside so Jane couldn't hear him. "This is a fixer-upper. And at the asking price, we couldn't afford to do that, even if we did know how."

Relieved to be removed from the sad atmosphere, we stood on the little front porch, sheltered behind its elephant ear vine. "How much land would there be?" Barry asked Jane, practising the form of a serious potential buyer, even when we both knew we were not going to buy this house.

"The house goes with about four acres. I can show you the deed, if you're interested."

"Is that a pump," asked Barry, "right out there on the lawn?"

"I was hoping you wouldn't ask about that," sighed Jane. When it came time to replace the pump that was one of the things Horace decided—to have the pump outside with the well. Of course, I'm sure it could be changed."

We rode back on the ferry, staying in the car this time because the rain was becoming heavier, saddened by the memory of the sorrowful old man, and of a fine house in a beautiful place, which we simply couldn't envision working for us.

After a long winter in which we continued to search, I discovered that what I had imagined would be a fine adventure turned out to be a lot less fun than I had expected. We hadn't realized how much sadness and loss we would encounter, how much we would feel like interlopers. Downsizing, old age, divorce. As we investigated more houses, seeing into owners' lives was tough. At the same time, in the back of our minds we knew we couldn't afford to go on being choosy forever. Maybe we would have to learn to settle for less. I remembered a lesson I had learned long ago.

In our twenties, when we were desperate to return to the Cobden farm community where we felt we belonged, Barry and I spent a whole summer hunting along country roads for somewhere to live with our baby son. Finally, in late August, bitterly disappointed by our failure to find any house to rent, we settled for renting a large, elegant, first floor apartment in the nearby town of Pembroke, which fronted on a busy street. It was all we could do, we told ourselves, but at that point we were feeling irrationally rejected by our chosen community. Sorrowfully we began preparing to move.

"In town, eh?" Our farmer friend Alva had dropped by the night we signed the lease. His raised craggy eyebrows said more than his words. We started to blather to him about the practical features, how much sense it made to live close to a hospital when you had a toddler, and how, try as we had, we simply couldn't find anywhere in the country to rent. He thought for a few minutes without commenting, then he asked, "Would you just consider coming out with me to look at a house I know of? It's only one line over from here — not fixed up, mind. Maybe it wouldn't be what you two would want at all. But you could have a look, anyway. See what you think." Alva took us in his big old boat of a Pontiac, driving slowly the long way around the block as if to point out just how precious the surrounding farm country was. In the setting sun, he drove down a long, tree-shadowed lane to a very old brick house, sheltered by a graceful, spreading elm. Nimbly, he bent and plucked the key from under the wooden stoop and took us in through the summer kitchen. He was right. This house was very old. Likely originally it had been log that subsequently had been bricked over, he remarked casually. The only heat sources were a small woodstove in the huge kitchen and an oil space heater in the dim living room. Upstairs were three bedrooms, with windows looking out across spreading fields and sweet little hills and distant, dark evergreen forests. When I raised a sash, I felt wrapped in blessed quiet.

There was only cold water in the kitchen tap, but Alva thought the landlord could be persuaded to stretch to the luxury of putting in a water heater for us since we had a baby. "Now, the outhouse— some people don't like that kind of thing. They need more, I guess." After Alva finished pointing out potential problems, he stared straight at both of us with his piercing blue eyes. "I know what I would do—if it was me..." And we knew what we had to do too. The ratty wallpaper, the two-seater outhouse didn't matter. We didn't even need to discuss it. Seeing the secluded house and the generous surrounding land, we felt peace stirring in us. There was no question that this was where we were meant to be.

That year, in spite of fierce cold and high drifting snow, and trips along the narrow tunnel we carved through mountainous snowbanks to reach the outhouse, and Saturday baths in a tub by the kitchen woodstove, we prospered. Over the year we gathered friends around us until the immense kitchen filled with music and rang with laughter, discovered the land in long walks, loved each other, and raised a baby.

So many times on this difficult journey, I thought to myself: "If only someone would help us as Alva had so long ago. If only we had someone to go with us — someone who knew more than we do." As we continued our search, one memory particularly came back to me. Strong, assured and capable, my mother took pride in finding romantic, interesting homes for her family. As a child, I remember that she could and did make a home for us anywhere, relishing the challenges of setting up in summer rentals or tents for camping. What I remembered now, though, was the way she heartened me in my first search in an unfamiliar city for an apartment after my marriage in the 1960s. With the utmost resourcefulness, she guided me, asking agents, scanning ads, questioning cashiers at corner stores. Her enthusiasm was infectious and kept me going long after I might have given up. "There will be a place for you. There always is. Don't give up. Don't settle for less. You just have to keep looking for a while. Isn't this fun? Who knows where you'll end up, but that's part of it. Just look at that wonderful big window, how it catches the sun. Maybe you can find something like that." These were the words I needed to hear, and within a couple of days we did indeed find a likeable two-storey apartment at the back of a handsome brick house.

Meanwhile, as I scanned more real estate ads, a mocking inward voice kept telling me that time was rushing ahead, and that we were getting nowhere. As we continued our frustrating search, always looking, thinking, imagining, we kept revising our wish list. Could we live there? We tried to imagine a new community, a new garden, a hospitable place for shelter, work, for gathering family and friends.

It was early June, and I wandered out under the cottonwood trees that sheltered the front of the park house to do some thinking. The most troublesome question continued to be how much would we need. After so little success in finding a suitable home, I knew we needed to think very carefully about what was necessary and what we could do without. We couldn't help hearing whispers from friends that maybe we wanted too much. After all, my concert-level pianist grandmother had kept her piano in an unheated sun porch, the only available space for it, and had worn a winter coat and galoshes so she could play the Liszt and Mendelssohn that she loved. Would I, could I, do the same?

I had been brought up in a family where simple living was accepted as a way to make possible precious things like books, musical instruments, and artist supplies. My father described his own grandparents' table as "Mennonite bare," unfinished wood that was scoured daily and both my parents were masters at contriving useful things from very little. In my artist parents' two-storey studio, my mother made and hung theatrical ceiling-to-floor curtains of white monk's cloth, which concealed makeshift cardboard drawers, each with its front painted a neat grey. But limited as they were, somehow they always found money to buy high quality oil and water colour paints.

I moved from the cottonwoods to sit on the steps of the back porch, my eyes blurring as I watched dragonflies dancing over the ripe, waving fieldgrass. As she did every spring, the phoebe was staring at me with dark eyes from her nest inside the porch roof. As I sat there, I was wrestling with the vexed question of how much was enough. I knew only too well how crippling it was to live in too small a space. When we first moved to the supervisor's house at Foley Mountain, I well remembered making my way miserably round and round the tall stacks of boxes that were hampering my unpacking. This is impossible, I thought. We just can't fit here. Indeed, there was only one closet for the whole house. Before we moved in we had imagined that we could squeeze ourselves into this house. Living in the park would certainly be worth it. We knew that. The trouble was that as little boys grew bigger, so did their snow boots, their coats, and indeed all their paraphernalia. By a remarkable stroke of good luck, eventually the Conservation Authority built a two-storey addition for us, which entirely changed the way we lived, making everything easier, expanding my sense of the possible, and giving Barry and me essential spaces of privacy so we could be happy both being together and separately pursuing our different interests. Having the addition also made much more feasible the taking in of family and friends at times of crisis, something I will always remember with thankfulness.

Once again, I revisited every feasible real estate website, once again ratcheting up the amount of money we would be prepared to spend. As I saw our limited nest egg, our precious inheritances from both families, dwindle and our security for the future ebb away, I shivered in spite of the steamy day. We already knew that our search for a home had come at an unfortunate time when housing prices were rising rapidly. Only later did we learn that our need for a home was coinciding with the first rush of a group of retiring baby boomers who were much better equipped to afford country places than we were. Many of these people were selling city properties for an impressive profit and moving to the country, where prices were comparatively cheap for them. Unlike us, many of them also were bolstered by generous pensions. Moreover, with the new restrictions on agricultural land, by the time we were searching, many farmers had severed as often as they legally could. After a number of years when rural prices had remained relatively stable, we had entered the market at a time when competition was intense and prices were rising at record rates.

It was not until late autumn that year, when Henry Connor offered to act as our own real estate agent, that we congratulated ourselves that we finally had the help we needed. Over an introductory lunch he assured us, "I am here to help you two clarify your ideas." Although his fading hair and beard made him appear vague, and I suspected that his musical voice had been artificially cultivated, all the same, we sensed something pouncing and tenacious under the surface. "Your job, now," our new adviser told us, "is to figure out exactly what you think you want and make a list for me. Then I will take you out to practise. That way I can get the feel of what you want. No obligations, mind," he said smoothly. "But this may help you to understand your needs better too."

And so, as soon as we returned home from our meeting with Henry, honed by all the unsatisfactory properties we had viewed, we sat down together and made our list. "As naturalists and writers, having wild and/or rural (farm) surroundings is a priority for us," Barry wrote down. "Ideally we would like an abandoned farm of thirty to one hundred acres, with a combination of woods, fields and wetlands. However, in the right setting, e.g. adjacent to Crown Land or surrounded by farms, we might be willing to consider a treed lot of three acres." We noted that although we were looking for an older house that was structurally sound, we needed it to have up-to-date wiring, heating, insulation and septic.

"Why not get something old and fix it up?" we were asked many times. "You could save yourselves so much money." Unfortunately, we knew that with our lack of renovation skills, work commitments and our age, a *handyman's special* would not work for us.

"What about the windows?" Already I was suspecting that one important challenge would be finding a house with the ones we hoped for. When we stayed at friends' houses where there were larger windows than the ones at the park house, we blossomed, feeling full of hope and imagination. As we got older, and probably more homebound, surely the sense of spaciousness and light from looking out would only become more necessary.

As for the house itself, we thought we could manage with about fifteen hundred square feet, three bedrooms and one bathroom, though we added that "larger is fine." Where most retired people were downsizing, we knew that space would be important to us. "We have an extensive book and art collection, so a good option for us would be a house where some rooms could be closed off to provide storage without additional heating costs or the property has a storage shelter in good condition."

"What about a new house?" I asked, just as Barry was putting away his note pad. "A new house would mean less maintenance." Setting aside the white frame farmhouse with gables, possibly decorated with wooden lace gingerbread, I envisioned a long, dark, brown-stained house with many windows, nestled snugly into a hill, perhaps. "Do you know how much a new house would cost?" Barry exclaimed. "We'd never be able to afford one."

This time, with a professional to guide us, we were on the right track at last. Forget the fears of being forced to live in a less than homelike place. After the holiday, with the help of our new agent, things should be fairly simple. We'd go to see a variety of houses in the company of an expert. Because of the time we had spent considering our wishes so carefully, we would narrow the search down to a few. Meanwhile, it might be interesting to see inside the prospects. "Sooner or later," Henry had assured us as he shook hands in parting, "there is a right house for everyone. Even if you don't think it's possible, I have to tell you that I've seen it happen over and over again." Here at last was the help we so badly needed.

Shortly before we were to go out with Henry, I took some time to sit in my favourite chair in the little room we called The Music Room, because it housed our piano and parlour organ. I was thinking about hope, and how much we needed it in our search, and I was remembering the only time when I almost gave up on it.

It was the first week in January, and the anniversary of the unforgettable ice storm of 1998. Where most freezing rain lasts for a few hours, in that terrible storm more than eighty hours of freezing rain imprisoned everything in glassy ice. Because of fallen trees and icy roads, transportation became treacherous. The buildup of ice snapped hydro poles and even crumpled pylons, causing massive, long-lasting power outages over a very wide area. At its height, more than two hundred and fifty communities in Ontario and Québec were declared a disaster. The military was called in to help clear debris, provide medical assistance, evacuate residents, and canvass door-to-door to make sure people were safe.

In most urban areas power was restored in a matter of days, but many rural communities suffered for much longer, and in fact, because of the isolation of our home in the park, it would take seventeen long days before our lights flickered back on. This was when, more than ever before, we were thankful for the great kindness of the people in our special little village. At first, staring through thickly glazed windows at a desolate world, listening to the endless crashing of trees, we felt a terrifying isolation. In the beginning we had no heat, no way of cooking, and not even a cell phone. In fact, it would be several days before a lumber skidder smashed its way along the park road so we could get out. However, although everyone, everywhere, needed help, we were never forgotten. At considerable risk from falling trees, men snowmobiled in to check on us and, as they became available, to lend us increasingly powerful generators that helped to keep our basement relatively dry as the days dragged on. Electricians, volunteer firemen, friends and people we had never met, old and young, all came to make sure we were safe and to help us.

In cities, while there was no power to run equipment, people without cash were turned away, but when Barry walked into Westport the merchants let him buy batteries, candles, and even a barbecue on the honour system. "We know where to find you," they joked. What was more, as soon as we could travel again, those whose power already had been restored overwhelmed us with invitations for hot showers and meals. Several kind families even invited us to bring our pets and move in with them for the duration.

But it was not the personal hardships I was remembering as I sat in the music room. If you love trees, a major ice storm breaks something in your heart. The heavy ice sheets toppled millions of trees, and indeed, because of the damage, more continued to break and fall for the rest of the winter. Before our eyes, our precious forest fell apart—friends, relatives, great spirits were shattered.

By the next week, once the work of surviving and starting to reopen the park had settled into a rhythm, we set out to walk the Beaver Pond Trail, the most familiar and most-loved of all the park trails. Because of the horrible masses of downed limbs, we had expected heavy going, but as we waded through chest-high fallen branches we actually were reeling, disoriented by a place where every familiar landmark was gone. No longer was there any way to tell where the much-travelled trail had gone. As we stumbled to a shocked halt, a doe who also was confused by the chaos bumped into us. This literally was entering a war zone, and for the first time I had a humbling sense of how living with war must feel.

Since a forest is an intricately entwined community, there was no certainty of what the future might hold. Moreover, already we had been warned by tree experts that the attrition from this profound ecological stress would continue for at least a decade because this storm-weakened forest now was much more vulnerable. With the trees' complicated dynamic systems weakened, from now on they would be more susceptible to assaults such as high winds. Eventually, it took the lumber skidder to clear the park road and a government crew to reopen the trails. But, as victims of the ice storm, the park trees were like war veterans limping home. Yes, they were still upstanding, but we knew many would never fully heal.

For a while, seeing the seeming fragility of nature and living with an unprecedented number of dead and dying trees drove home how easily a landscape could be changed for the duration of human memory. And, for a while, this shook me badly. In a crisis of faith soon after the nightmarish attempt to walk the Beaver Pond Trail, I suggested to Barry that I might stop writing about nature and switch completely to writing fiction. How could I justify celebrating nature when I was only too aware of how damaged it was becoming, in part because of human greed? Surely this terrible storm was only a foreshadowing of the environmental devastation that already was becoming apparent. And yes, I was only too aware that, in spite of my best efforts, I continued to be part of the problem.

Some of my personal healing began with our experience of the kindness of an entire village. But also, with time, I could not help seeing that in the midst of the destruction there still was life, yes, life everywhere. The generation of brave or desperate Irish farmers, struggling to carve out lives for themselves and their families on what was known as "the mountain" had learned that the land where I lived was what was known as a starve acres. The trees that survived harsh conditions to thrust out of the granite rock were broad, but not tall, distorted in many ways. But were they not more wonderful because of their resilience? Perhaps, I began to think, it started with the smallest things, the soil, ironically now nurtured by a wealth of fallen branches, the seedlings sprouting from sheltered crevices, the survival of storm-shaped pines. As I refocussed on the preciousness of what was left, and as I began to see nature regenerate, I renewed my commitment to hope. The privilege of living closely with Foley Mountain reminded me that it was important to continue to write appreciatively of nature, damaged as it might be, for as long as I was able.

On a bleak Saturday in January we met Henry to begin the process of finding the house that we hoped and believed was out there waiting for us. Our search began with an hour's drive to the north, a chance, our agent said, for us to get to know each other better. "You'll like Henry. He's different, and he's effective," said the friends who had recommended him to us. Indeed, he was very different from the other agents we met. For one thing, he was the most Dickensian man I have ever encountered. His odd, self-admitted love of words sprang up at the strangest moments. For example, there were his unwelcome variations on herons as "unpleasant, unlovable birds, of use to nobody" which carried us past miles of frozen swamps and massive rock cuts. In between his monologues though, he listened. Henry was exquisitely interested in what we might want and in teaching us to look ourselves. Under other circumstances, I might have loved his enthusiasm for and knowledge of house restoration and antiquity. However, when I was sitting in the messy rear seat of his old station wagon, it was always in the back of my mind that he used to be involved in theatre. Certainly his long preambles and patter of carefully chosen words were wearing and confusing. Although we couldn't be sure, his verbiage might even have been intended to set up a fog.

Over the course of the morning we learned about side-splits and other forms of split-level houses, and how you couldn't necessarily gauge the size of a house from outside. Some homes were bigger inside than we could have guessed, while others were surprisingly cramped. We easily rejected a house with dank tobacco smells, one with fake marble fireplaces, and one with many narrow, steep flights of stairs, and were quite definite in saying "No" to one with a four foot high crawl space to get at the fuse box.

Could we find a way to fit our things in? What did we need to get rid of? These were questions that often surfaced to goad us. Friends frequently reproached us for having too many things. Most retired people threw out most of their possessions, they pointed out. We knew that. And they might have asked how exactly did owning a lot of possessions fit in with our wish to live a simple life? The answer was that, being committed to living in the country, we always leaned towards self-reliance, and self-reliance meant tools, storage, and, yes information and amusements. Examining my possessions felt to me like the Water Rat in *The Wind in the Willows,* describing the wondrous contents of his picnic basket. As a long-time weaver and spinner, I had accumulated two floor looms, two spinning wheels, a sewing machine, much-used for mending as well as creative endeavours, and a wealth of yarns and fabric. I also owned, and loved, a large, old-fashioned piano and also a parlour organ, which lingered on simply because nobody else wanted it.

Our biggest difficulty, though, if also our glory, was our passion for books and reading. Thanks to my inheritances and many library sales, we owned hundreds of books. For years I also relied on libraries, but recently, as I witnessed the dissolution of collections of many invaluable books and old favourites, I knew I would want to keep our own ones safe and near me for what I hoped would be many years to come. As a country writer with wide-ranging interests, who lived far from urban libraries, I never knew what references I might want to access quickly. Just as the Water Rat's beloved river felt like meat and drink to him, so did our book collection feel to us. Our rural life would feel much poorer without tools and books and music.

By now it was late in the day, and we wanted nothing more than to be allowed to go back to our own home at Foley Mountain while it still was our home. "Listen," appealed Henry, although he surely was aware that we were tired and disappointed. "Just humour me with one more property. This one is a brick house, a farmhouse, just as you wanted. The owner was an old lady who lived there all her life, and she has just died." For an hour we drove west into the setting sun, in a state of grinding irritation, hearing the clashing of gears every time we turned to another back road. As he drove, our real estate agent preserved a thoughtful silence, and we weren't inclined to pursue our real estate theory studies further.

"But this is right on the highway," I protested, as we drove down a long driveway, littered with ugly farm sheds. "We said no highways," Barry reproached Henry. We knew immediately that we would not even consider this house, situated on flat, treeless land, with the constant sound of traffic obscuring any bird sound. Leaving the agent exclaiming over an interesting old enamelled cookstove, which we had no doubt he would snap up later from the heirs for a pittance, Barry and I stumped back to the station wagon to talk things over.

After our outing with Henry, we were beginning to question whether we knew what we wanted. We had thought we felt most at home in comfortable old farmhouses. Yet the many awkward little rooms we so often found in these felt inhospitable. Worse still, we knew large windows and good views were important to us, yet the farmhouses we investigated all had small windows. Although we were not ready to admit it, we were beginning to suspect that to get what we wanted we would need a more modern house.

"There, wasn't that fun," gloated Henry after returning us to our starting point in the twilight at the end of the long day. But after we parted with him, on our drive back to the park, all I could think of was that when I walked inside an unlikeable house, I felt like a shell-less snail: raw, vulnerable, and shrinking.

I am still puzzled about why we came away from our last of several futile outings with Henry feeling like bad children who had disappointed his well-laid plans. Although we did learn from our agent, he never showed us a house that we thought was at all possible. All the same, his last prediction remained to haunt us: "Believe me, I've sold many houses in my time, and the one thing I can guarantee—in fact, this is a stock phrase in our trade, I can assure you—is that the house you end up in won't be the one you set out to find. You will be surprised. Trust me: that I know for certain."

The "adventure" of looking for our own home had turned to grinding, worrying work. For all our jousting with Henry, by now I think we both harboured the fear that his predictions would come true, and that eventually we would have to settle for so much less that we would be unhappy for the rest of our years. As the weeks slipped by, it was hard not to lose heart.

There were many reasons for us to feel scared. After all, in a sense, Henry's assessment of us was right. At almost sixty, we were completely inexperienced at home buying. Certainly, before our years at the park, we had hunted more or less successfully for a series of rented homes. But when we rented, we always knew that if something went wrong, fixing it would be the landlord's responsibility. If all else failed, we could always move.

Although we certainly were learning as we went along, we had too much invested in this search, and we were aware that we had very little latitude for error. Mistakes could be disastrous. What if we closed too soon, for example, settling for less, and then found something we liked better? Because so much was at stake, every cautionary story we heard made us panic.

Just one example of the possible risks facing homeowners was the experience of nearby friends, who were hotly contesting a threatened mine. "We were only gone for a week, and when we came home, there were test pits dug everywhere. The prospectors came right on our land without permission and without warning. Unbelievably, there is no protection for us in the law. We knew we didn't own the mining rights. Hardly anyone does around here. But it just never occurred to us that prospectors could behave like that. Can you imagine trucks thundering down our little back road all the time! If they go ahead, we'll have to move. But what kind of compensation would there be for us then?"

In our search, already we had driven along once-lovely side roads, curving between rolling hills, now disfigured by working sand and gravel pits. What if we found a place to love, only to have one of these erupt nearby, shattering the peace and beauty of the land, possibly even harming the water table?

People were only too quick to warn us too about neighbourhood feuds, about prohibitively expensive fences, which were forced because of border disputes, about big trees cut down without permission.

In our hearts we knew that there were no guarantees, that we would have to live with uncertainty, appreciating every good moment of life. We knew that we wanted this home of our own terribly, perhaps too much. Sometimes, within me I heard a hurtful voice: "And what if you do find it? Will you be happy then, or will you simply be emptied out? After so many years of loving wandering the many trails of Foley Mountain, will you ever be able to live fully anywhere else?"

As we persevered, on our own once again, one of the things I clung to was a story I heard one day in a doctor's waiting room. I mentioned to the trim woman sitting beside me there that we were looking for a house. (I said this to everyone I met, hoping somehow, someone would know of the right place for us.) "Oh, I know what that's like. I've just been through it," the woman, Margaret, surprised me by saying. "It'll all work out. You'll see." Before I could protest she went on, "All you have to remember is that sometimes you try too hard. Sometimes you have to back off and not work at it so much. That's what happened to me." She gave me a kindly nod of encouragement.

"After I retired, I went out with agents looking so many times, that I was thoroughly discouraged, I can tell you. Then," her voice brightened, "I just took a day off, and went for a drive in a part of Lanark that was new to me. I wasn't looking for a place to live that time. Quite the opposite. I didn't really care where I went and I wasn't paying attention, just enjoying the fall day. Well, because I wasn't keeping track of where I was going, I have to admit that I got a little bit lost and ended up down a dead-end road. That was when I noticed the hand-painted *for sale* sign.

"And, can you believe it, this turned out to be the perfect house and land for me. It had absolutely everything I could have wanted and more, and the price was right too. I bought it the very next day and I've been happy ever since."

"Remember," she said, turning back to me as she followed the nurse into the doctor's office, "don't try too hard. It'll happen when it's time. You see if it doesn't."

By August of the second year of our search we had viewed more than eighty properties and most local real estate agents knew us on a first name basis. Having spent far too much time on us already, they were slow to return our calls. When we did connect, not surprisingly, their handshakes were less hearty. We knew more about assessing a house's structure than we would ever have imagined possible. We knew that sometimes new houses, although unattractive from the outside, were spacious and comfortable within. We had a much better idea of what we could live with. Sadly, we were nowhere close to finding the home and land we could love as we loved living at Foley Mountain.

In the end, though, just as Margaret had predicted, the results of our search were not in our hands at all. And I always will be convinced that the country home of our heart's desire was waiting for us all along.

II

Falling in Love

Ａnd then, just when we had nearly given up hope, we fell in love. In all the months we searched, we had never found a single place that felt close to right. Patiently, over and over, we repeated to ourselves, and anyone else who would listen, that what mattered most to us were the surroundings. We were willing to compromise over the house, but we needed a parcel of land that we could care for. But land, it seemed, was the hardest thing to find. To our sorrow, we now knew that large properties were beyond us, but nowhere could we turn up any homes surrounded by smaller, more affordable acreages. All the houses that interested us had been severed from working farms and came with only a single acre of land.

In late August, goaded by the anxious thought that our lead-time was slipping away from us, I mechanically investigated the few fresh properties that were being listed, and phoned real estate agents, and pleaded with them to keep us in mind. Then, on a breezy late-summer day, Barry took an afternoon off work so we could explore a new direction, west of our present home. Travelling on an appealing narrow country road bordered by old farms and oak forests, we came to a neat, modern brick bungalow with a homemade "for sale" sign nailed to a tree in front of it. When the young owner brought us in to see it, the new, solid, clean house was exemplary, with many features we appreciated, including a heat pump, propane gas appliances, and a main-floor craft room. But for all that, we simply didn't like the place. The only reasonable objection we could give to the anxious owner was that the living room was a windowless one in a finished basement.

While Barry went with the owner to inspect the useful, large workshed that blocked the view from the kitchen window, I wandered off to see what kind of walks might be available. Cresting a little hill in the small back yard, I halted. Right behind what would be the property line of the treed one-acre lot was a hunt camp with all its untidy paraphernalia, including a hanging rack and dog kennels. "Oh you wouldn't need to worry about this," said the owner, who had hurried up behind me. "My brothers and me are going to move the camp further back. It wouldn't be there when you bought the place." Feeling more discouraged than ever, we declined the house and headed back to the park.

For the first year of our search we had played at imagining that our new home must be just around the corner, waiting for us. By this time, although we were no longer so hopeful, investigating all signs had become routine, so when I spotted an unusually large real estate *Lots for Sale* sign further up the road, I said to Barry: "It's a lovely afternoon, and it would be a shame to go back home so early. Why don't we drive down to have a look?" Seeing the familiar look of objection on his face I added hastily, "We both know we are not going to buy a building lot. But this must be the only road so close to home that we've never explored before. Why don't we follow it a bit? That way the day won't feel so wasted."

Barry drove slowly down a steep hill and onto a twisty little dirt road, bordered by a spreading marsh on one side and a farm of fine rolling fields on the other. Unspoken, was our secret wish that this would be the time when our home would spring out at us as it had for Margaret, the woman who told me her story in the waiting room. A few miles along what was scarcely more than a dirt track, the township road signs were replaced by a white one, on which was painted in red: *Private Road: Use at your own risk*. Venturing on, we passed a hilltop line of fifteen huge maples, backed by a ragged old rail fence. Used as we were to the sorrow of seeing ice storm damaged trees in and near the park, we had almost forgotten the pleasure of seeing trees with such large crowns. Soon, the road swooped close by a lake, giving us a long view of distant islands and more tree-clad hills. We came to a crossroads where a further large sign showed "lake estates" both straight ahead and to the right. "We're *not* building a house," Barry warned me. "We can't even think of it. Everyone says building is a money pit. You know as well as I do that it's out of the question for us." I knew he was right.

And yet we continued, driving up a steep hill, sheltered by a forest of hemlocks and yellow birch. Seeing the generous lots here, which were marked off by numbers on trees, I couldn't help imagining owning part of this lovely forest. Still, I, who had grown up enclosed by trees, hungered for somewhere more open to spend my last days. Yes, there would have to be trees, interesting, varied trees, but now I envisioned somewhere I could watch the path of sun, moon, and stars and spend hours simply studying passing clouds. We went back down the hill and turned onto the right-hand fork and drove to the end of a dead-end road.

"This is the sweetest land in the whole area," I whispered as we loitered, looking far over a lake dotted with many islands. "What a farm it must have been before it was divided. We always said we wanted to live on a dead-end road like this," I couldn't help adding. "No. I know. We can't even think of building."

Nevertheless, a few days later I was not surprised when Barry brought home a green real estate lot map along with the news that there was one back lot that was selling for very little. "I suppose it wouldn't hurt just to look," he told me. Before the week was out, we returned, drawn as by a magnet to the exceptionally beautiful land.

From the map we learned that all the lots were surprisingly large, varying from thirteen to fifty acres. The eight expensive lakefront lots were nearly all sold, but what remained were some larger "back lots," away from the lake. These were marked as "access lots" because, as well as the land, each offered joint ownership of a stretch of land along a bay of the lake.

Later that same afternoon we found ourselves searching out the faded pink-painted stakes marking the boundaries of the inexpensive lot, which turned out to be very near the road's end. However, when we established the front line for this we were disappointed. A steep driveway would be required to reach what we thought was the only house site, and the land itself was strewn with boulders that would make it poor for walking. No. "Just throw that away." Barry crumpled the green map and flung it on the floor of the car. "Let's walk back along this farm lane while we're here, and then we'll call it quits."

Curving away from the road beyond the disappointing bargain lot, we came out on an enclosed winding valley, backed by a high, tree-clad wall of a hill. "That view is everything we ever dreamed of," I breathed.

"Somebody is going to be awfully lucky," Barry added.

We stood for a long while, simply looking at the magnificent valley. Then, on the way back to the car, I stumbled upon a mossy spring, bubbling out of the rocky hillside and surrounded by tall ostrich ferns. Imagine: land that could sustain a spring during this summer of serious drought. Indeed, this exceptional, set-apart place must be blessed with groundwater and good soil because the trees looked healthy and green here unlike most on the rocky lands nearby.

In spite of our reservations about building, the area so near to and yet so far from Foley Mountain haunted us. Back home, in spite of myself, I smoothed the green map and studied it again until I found another back lot that might be affordable. On the weekend, we returned to search for more of the maddeningly obscure pale pink-painted stakes, pacing out boundary lines.

Tempted off the road, I slipped into a little woods and down a small deer path to a perfect clearing rimmed by forest. The far, northern edge of this lot was bordered by a little ravine, sheltered by some fine large maples. Beyond that, the trail led down to the valley. "Now this is more like it," exclaimed Barry, when he joined me. Too in love with the land to leave, we followed the deer path further down a small, sloping hill and into the glorious, sheltered meadow that stretched the length of the valley. Just how far back would this lot go? We had no idea what the stated twenty acres might include. Unfortunately, though, when we reached the edge of the meadow, it seemed our path was blocked. The lovely far-reaching field turned out to be a water meadow. Even in this drought summer, walking across the hummocky wetland was nearly impossible. It appeared sure that the back half of the lot would be virtually inaccessible. We abandoned the search for more survey stakes, and went home.

Then fate, in the shape of our teacher son, intervened. Morgan had been phoning frequently to see what properties we were turning up. This time, when Barry told him about the lot we had found, he offered to come on Sunday to see the land with me. While Barry stayed home to do paperwork, Morgan and I went together to explore. Nobody could be a better companion than the ever-enthusiastic Morgan. This time, walking the land together, we discovered something that made the place much more feasible and desirable. I had not noticed that the green real estate map showed the lot widening significantly mid-way back. Now, when Morgan and I discovered the mid-point boundaries down in the valley, we could see this broadening. It turned out that at the base of the hill closest to the house site, we could easily skirt around a little island of trees, and meet up with the farm lane where it curved through the valley on slightly higher ground. What this meant was that the lot actually included an easy way to bypass the river of tall grass and water and reach the farm lane that threaded through the entire valley.

Elated by our discovery, we set out to walk the whole length of the meadow. Before long, beside the lane we came to a tiny pond, a shimmering piece of reflected sky in the midst of grassland. This too would be yours, Morgan pointed out. "Ours. Think about it!" We tramped on, leaving the lane to walk through the field to a handsome solitary burr oak, a single large tree standing like a guardian in the midst of the low land. Pausing here to savour the views of the long, winding valley and its surrounding forest-clad hills, we scared up a marsh wren, its short tail whisking in displeasure at our intrusion. Beneath the oak's craggy branches we discovered shaggy capped acorns very unlike those of the red and white oaks we were familiar with. I began to see that living here would bring different kinds of natural experiences from those at the park. Although we would lose daily contact with aspects we loved, there would be new discoveries.

Stretching high over the meadow we found that "our" lot included a steep hill, which I impulsively named Box Hill, after the English one visited by Jane Austen's Emma Woodhouse and her companions. Ascending this, we discovered that "our" acreage included part of a woodland, with a few impressive ancient maple and ash trees. Surveying the meadow from the crown of the hill, I was amazed by the spread of land. Much of this would be ours, I thought in wonder, although actually I do not believe anyone can own land. It "belongs" to all beings. But we could be stewards, and this was an exciting possibility for people who had always lived on others' properties. "Mom," Morgan told me as we descended the hill, "You two will be crazy if you pass up this chance."

"You'll know," people had told us. "When it's the right place for you, you'll know." One dear friend had gone so far as to say that our future home was already waiting for us. And now, we were finding that this was true. As it turned out, the feeling of finding home was more profound than excitement. It was a heartfelt knowing, a not being able to leave it behind.

The next Friday morning, Barry and I returned by ourselves, determined to have one more look around. When I showed him how you could bypass the wetland to walk freely around what could be our land, and then how it went wider than we had imagined and stretched much farther as well, he also was impressed by the beauty and range of the lot. For the first time in months, it was raining and we stalked around with damp pant legs, considering potential house sites. Not daring to push too hard, I urged, "All I know is that I would be terribly disappointed if someone bought it before we had a chance to decide." Thanksgiving was coming, when all the leaf peepers from the city would converge on the country. It seemed very likely that someone with more money and decision would snap "our lot" up, and this was the only access lot we would want. We both knew that. In a strange, dreamlike way it felt as if things were falling into place in ways we could never have imagined. Then, ominously, as we were driving away, we caught sight of a man studying the lot plan on the signboard for the development.

We would just wander into Westport to Terry Bryan's real estate office to investigate further about lot lines, we told ourselves. When we dashed in through the rain, so long desired and now pouring down, it turned out that our long-time friend Neil Scott was working in the office. "If it was what I wanted," he said slowly and thoughtfully, apparently as much to himself as to us, "I would make an offer. I wouldn't wait for someone else to take it—if I was really certain that it was what I wanted, that is. I don't think there is much to lose. You put your money down and you write in all the conditions you need to feel safe." I held my breath. "Could you write that up for us now?" asked Barry. Neil pulled out a piece of paper from his desk drawer and jotted down everything we wanted—well tests, hydro installed. We went home in a speechless, disbelieving daze.

That night, trying to make the amazing prospect real to myself, I wrote to a friend:

> There are many miles of farmer-owned fields, forest and ponds, where we believe we would be allowed to walk. The lake people will doubtless build near the lake, which means we will look out on unspoiled forest and meadow, never seeing them. Some of these people also bought one or two back lots to ensure their privacy, so we will have even more unspoiled land. If we are successful buying the lot, we'll hold it for a year and then get a prefab home built to our design just before Barry's retirement. We are both looking forward to designing a house to suit us. I envision it hanging over the meadow in the valley…

Quite quickly, our offer was countered. "They're not giving much," said Neil, who had already expressed exasperation with the owners. We countered back, and then we could only wait.

What ever were we thinking of? The one thing we *said* we could never do, would never do, was to build. We had been so firm in this decision. Everyone had told us that putting yourself in the hands of contractors was the slippery road to a hell of delays, cost overruns, disappointments and misunderstandings. How many times had we heard a real estate agent point out that you always got "a lot more house" when you bought an existing building? The quality of materials and workmanship in these was often better, harking back to times when supplies were far cheaper. While we waited, we comforted ourselves with the idea that we could control the quality of materials and construction if we built. What was more, a brand new house would give us years without further expense and surprise.

Privately, I wondered whether there mightn't be pleasure along the way. Building was in my blood. My father's ancestors had lived by building houses, and I remembered Saturday morning visits with my father, gazing up tall ladders into sky-high rafters and scuffing the pine-scented piles of sawdust across the newly sawn floorboards. Looking down genially from a great height, my uncle, who worked with my grandfather, told me proudly how my grandmother, his mother, had won nail-driving contests at fairs. Much later, I inherited a number of interesting moulding planes from my father's collection, which had come from earlier generations of his family.

The following weekend when we went to the land, I galumphed about, checking for possible house-sites. On that fine morning, I felt dazzled by the place. The likeliest location for our home-to-be was open and looking out over the meadow. The trouble was that this was very near the border of the neighbouring lot. From there I went back to a cutaway filled with aspens, its sides built up with rocks. This spot, which had its own small, protected meadow, and would have a buffer of trees in front and to the sides of a house, appeared sheltered from the winds and to some degree protected from the summer sun. On the first day we came to this land, we had found pressed-down patches in the long grass, which told us that deer found this was a safe place for them to lie down. With careful thinning it could retain a forest and field feeling with a view of the big meadow and the guardian burr oak. "The door knocker," I grabbed Barry's arm in excitement, remembering the oak knocker we had bought earlier in Québec as a present for our future home. "That's it. Finding the knocker was right. The burr oak was waiting for us."

Sitting in the cool autumn sunshine on leaves of wild strawberries and violets, we ate the fruit and cheese I had grabbed up. Then we began a lighthearted search for back boundaries. Most wonderfully, when we finally followed our lot line to one of our back stakes in a forest of ironwoods, we discovered that we would own even more land than we expected. Barry went on to clamber down a steepish ridge, exploring further, while I decided to stay above, savouring my happiness. Staring up at the mahogany-coloured ash leaves, instinctively I began an informal inventory of all the plants, all the trees we would have, and even bittersweet vines, with berries as yet unkissed by frost. Each was precious.

We kept in touch by voice, and eventually Barry rejoined me, extremely excited. What he had discovered, he told me, was a large, full beaver pond with many rickety heron nests high in the dead trees there, as well as another shallower pond, ringed by rocky cliffs. Gazing at the sheet of still water, he wondered whether there was an easier way to get here from our field, rather than scrambling up and down the ridge, and indeed, by edging along the base of the hill he found he could reach the meadow in five minutes. But he also made a special discovery, a sunken opening of a small cave, protected by a rocky cliff, which was lush with ferns and mosses. Even in this dry year a spring welled up from the cave, only to disappear back underground soon after. After spending the day, he too was fired by the place. At last he was as delighted by the prospect of living here as I. Indeed, we found so much to explore that we lingered all afternoon. Before we left, because I couldn't help it, I poked around the front of the property sowing some acorns and pinecones I had collected from the park. I loved this place. I loved it.

A few days later, coming home to the park from buying groceries, I was tempted into a detour to slip over to see the land.

Although technically we didn't own it yet, a magnetic pull kept drawing me there. On the way I thought how, living at this new place, we would be within our familiar "circle of reference," just as we had wished to be. Living in our new home, we would be no further from our favourite towns of Perth and Kingston. What's more, just as we'd hoped, our new place would keep us close to our Westport friends.

As soon as I slipped out of the car beside our lot, I was pleased to discover a splendidly red-crested pileated woodpecker, and to see hosts of little sparrows in the valley's river of grass. While I stood beside the car watching the birds fluttering low over the abundant ripe seeds there, I felt the presence of a very different lake from the one I was used to. Now, for the first time, I let myself think beyond the land. Living here, we would be an easy five-minute saunter away from Bobs Lake, far closer than we presently were to the park beach on the Little Rideau Lake. Eager to stay a little longer, I decided to investigate the cottage lane, which began almost directly across from our land. Along the rough, narrow road, I passed a single cottage, and directly beyond this cottage and right beside the lane, I came upon a stretch of rocky shore, sheltered by impressive white cedars. Standing looking through the cedars I caught sight of a small flock of wild geese basking on the sunlit bay. Across on the far shore was the long tree-clad ridge, the "lake access" of which we would have shared ownership. Ahead of me the lane curved invitingly, travelling up and down hill, passing very tall bitternut hickories, their bark dappled with golden lichen, some ancient maples, and more fine oak trees. Before long I was back out on the development road, very nearly across from where the farm lane wound down into the valley. Standing by the road, I realized that in all the time I was there I had not heard the sound of a single vehicle.

Later that week, we learned that the vendors refused to move at all on their asking price. Nevertheless, in our hearts, we were in too deep now to give up. I think we both knew that, for better or worse, we were irrevocably committed to this twenty acres. We checked our offer to purchase with our lawyer and he confirmed that from his point of view it looked fine. Then, as soon as Barry finished teaching his class at the park and with only ten minutes to spare before its closing time, we rushed to the township office. Here we were presented with two large books of subdivision plans, filled with all kinds of studies of the soil. Flipping hurriedly through these, one for each of us, we noticed with some anxiety that the well depths and flow varied considerably over the development. There was, of course, no guarantee that we would achieve a good well without considerable extra expense.

One interesting thing we learned was that some of the waterfront sites had been declared archaeologically significant. What this meant was that if any artifacts were found during excavation, all work had to stop until the proper authorities assessed that location. From the first day, this beautiful lakeside land had felt to me like a place where First Nations people might have visited. Later, when we were settled, I hoped to find out more.

On the damp holiday Sunday of Thanksgiving, Morgan and his partner Rick met us over at the land so we could show Rick the place. The many maples were in the glory of their autumn colour, and, after the fall rains, the fields were startlingly green. Barry took us to see the grotto he had discovered deep in the woods, and on to the big back pond, where we counted the tufts of at least ten large heron nests. Judging by the location of one of the official metal survey stakes, we confirmed that we owned a small portion of the pond, which would allow us to put a canoe in or set up an observation blind as my favourite nature writer Edwin Way Teale had done. This "brushpile study", as he called it, was simply a mound of weathered sticks "about eight feet across and six and a half feet high" which gave him "a room with a hundred windows" through which he had an intimate view of the birds and creatures nearby.

At the pond we scared up a lingering heron and then a pair of distressed marsh hawks. My guess was that none of these birds normally saw people, so I felt particularly badly to have barged heedlessly into their sheltered world. Even when we returned to the meadow much later, the hawks were circling fretfully.

Across the pond, Barry also found a beaver's small bank burrow. While Barry and Rick talked about possibilities, Morgan and I walked on down the winding valley until we came to a rail fence and an alluring vista of more long, curving, forest-sheltered meadows. After we returned to our home at the park, surrounded by the celebratory fragrance of turkey, we pulled out our topographical map to get a better understanding of the fields Morgan and I had overlooked. Seeing the complex elevation lines ringing the many hills as well as the sheltered fields, we got a new sense of the possibilities for many wonderful hikes in the future.

And yet, I felt a stab of disloyalty to the park. "Do you think we really can be happy with what is here?" I asked Barry anxiously, sweeping my hand over the map. So long, and so intensely had I walked the beloved land at the park that I couldn't help wondering: could I ever give my heart to walking somewhere else? If Barry hadn't taken the supervisor's job at Foley Mountain, and we hadn't moved to the farmhouse that went with it, we likely would have been content simply to remain rural people. Likely we and our sons would not have known the feeling of being close to a fine variety of wild habitats, which included ridges with far vistas, pinewoods, rocky barrens, deep valleys, many different ponds, and even the shore of a lake.

When we turned away from Foley Mountain, we would be ripping up the thirty years of intimacy that had begun with our first hike in winter when we had found a recently shed deer antler lying on a mossy bank. Walking throughout the park in all seasons, we knew where the deer yarded in winter; we knew where the bear was likely to skirt our clearing in early spring; we knew of a mysterious straight line of butternuts that seemed as if it surely must follow a ley line; we knew places, such as groves of venerable shagbark hickory trees, which we were pretty sure no one living knew of. I even knew places to sit, such as a granite boulder in the woods, against which I could lean my backpack to shrug out of it easily, where there was a good smooth play area where a baby could safely crawl. When we left all this to go to our new land, we would become strangers in a strange land.

Soon after, Barry discovered a bit more of our new property's story. He had been in touch with a technician at Rideau Valley Conservation Authority, who told him that the "sweet farm" had been a problem for the developer owners since 1988. Originally, twice as many lots had been proposed but, in the consideration of septic systems and wells, the Conservation Authority had insisted on reducing the number because of the sensitivity of the land. She felt it would be a good place for us. "You should see it in summer, when the lake levels will be five feet higher."

When I hung up from our talk, I felt as close to rapture as I ever have. "At play in the fields of the Lord." I have always loved that phrase. And now it looks as if I might spend all my last years overlooking such a field, playing, roaming, discovering freely there for myself. Sitting on the back porch of the friendly old farmhouse that had been home to us for so many years, I asked: What am I here for?

To try to get a broader sense of who I am and where I need to go.
To regain rapture.
To learn to talk with God.

III

Time of Waiting

Friday began our building search with a likeable dealer specializing in prefab houses. After an hour with him, we felt that we just might end up with a home far closer to our dreams than we had dared imagine possible. Before we left, we wandered around his modest show room admiring possible wooden floors and tile and cabinets. The many people who came to visit our park house, which they knew as *the old McCann house,* told us that this was a home where they, or their family, had been happy. Certainly it had been a good home for us as well. However, with only one small bathroom, limited closets, a damp basement where salamanders felt happy, and a poorly insulated kitchen where I sometimes had to wear a winter hat and coat, living there was not comfortable. What we saw that day all looked better than we had expected, certainly better than what we were used to.

That night, however, we revisited our finances. The money the dealer suggested we might well need to spend would compromise us all of our lives. And yet living deeply, appreciatively, simply, was a life path we would always choose. Surely with care and thought we would still be able to do this.

On a morning soon after, I sat with my coffee by the kitchen window, watching flying clouds and putting down on paper what I would like in a house. I wanted to dream a while.

Inevitably, I turned first to the home where I grew up: a brown-stained, rustic house that had been part of its woodland environment, snugging into the surroundings. Remembering, I envisioned a flagstone or brick walk leading to a deck or verandah, with an entryway to the kitchen, and with steps down to a kitchen garden.

Windows. It always came down to windows. Glancing at the disappointing blank wall over our present kitchen sink, I put down "a decent kitchen window where I work." Then I jotted down "Two windows on different walls for our bedroom, and large ones for our living room," which would overlook a woodland glade in summer and would have a spreading view across the valley in winter, and finally, "a patio door downstairs to let in light and give a view of the flower beds I hope to make."

My bedroom at my childhood home had had a door opening into the woods, which meant that I could slip out into the woods whenever I wanted to. However, when I went away to Guide camp, I was charmed by something even better. The big army bell tent we slept in was always responsive to the weather. On hot August days we rolled up the sides so we had a floating shelter, open to every welcome breeze. And this was what I began to imagine for our new home: windows, which, when lifted, drew in all the summer winds.

As I mused, I began to see that for me one of the pleasures of this experience would be thinking about architectural design. I remembered discovering a new house so inspiring that it haunts me still. I came upon it when I was roaming the land near my Mississauga home as a girl. I wandered into a new subdivision, the back of which stretched along a narrow, forested ravine. Although in theory I furiously resented these encroachments on what I saw as my own wild preserves, in the construction stages I also found the new houses were fertile places to scavenge for interesting scraps — leftover tiles to make mosaics and useful bits of wood to carry back to my hideaway at the back of my parents' woods. On this autumn afternoon, I came upon the beginnings of a house unlike any I had ever seen, a house made almost entirely of glass. Slipping through the unlocked door, I found myself in a large open space floating over the ravine. Right then, and ever afterwards, I knew that this simple, elegant house, which I later learned was designed by architect Leo Venchiarutti for his own use, reflected the style I would want in a home.

As I wrote, I was thinking: "This is the place I was always moving towards. A home in closest relationship to the land." In a way, I had been preparing for this house all my life.

Meanwhile, what continued to surprise me was my strange, calm certainty that living on this land was what was meant for me. Sometimes I had a flash of recognition beyond reason. It was as if I had known this place all my life, and perhaps even before my own life. Time changed when I was there. I got echoes from my childhood, as if even then, deep inside, I had intimations that this wonderful place was waiting for me. When I was there, I felt utterly sure that this landscape was where I belonged.

Counting blessings there was easy. First was the blessing of quiet. This dead end hill farm country drew us in and nourished us with a rich, ripe silence. Here, there were only the rare, distant sounds of a passing train to break the peace. There were hills within hills. Curves and vistas abounded. It was a place of many springs. And on...

On a soft, mild Saturday in November, Barry and I packed small bakery quiches, grapes, apples, and Swiss cheese and went for one of our exploring trips to what would be our new area. First we made our way to the cedar-sheltered beach and found sculptured driftwood to take as a present to our land—two big stumps and two others like wings to put up on the house we were going to build. Gazing through the black-green lace of cedars, listening to the slap, slap of little waves, watching ducks bobbing across the bay, and discovering the driftwood lying on the rocky shore, felt like dwelling in Emily Carr country. We hid the pieces in our little front woods until we could use them. I loved bringing gifts of seeds, cones, acorns, and now the handsomely weathered, sculpted wood to our place.

Then we explored the land across the road from us and discovered a special sheltered ridge overlooking the lake where we sat under fine white oaks and ochre-budded bitternut hickories, their bark crusted with lichens, and listened to little waves breaking against the rocks in the bay below. Back at our house site for lunch, we caught ourselves gazing in delight over the long, winding valley and discussing future walks. Indeed, we congratulated ourselves that there were so many places to explore here that we hardly knew where to start, although winter was approaching, and we were not sure how much more we would be able to do before the snow came.

Only a week later, after a storm of driving rain followed by snow, we awoke early to sun and a radiant blue sky, swept by fleecy clouds. Barry burst in from feeding the park birds and suggested that on this rare, perfect wintry day we simply had to visit the land. And in the pure, clear, cold air it was exquisite there, with the prettiest possible views of fields and farms and trees mounded with snow. In a way, the expanses seemed broader, blanketed in pristine whiteness; in another, they had that muffled, bundled feeling of gathering one in to shelter.

We made our way to the spring that fed our tiny pond. There we watched the slow, secret welling of water from the cleft in the rocks. Thinking of birds, I wondered whether this water might possibly stay open in winter.

With childlike, joyful wandering, we returned to moon about at our house site until Barry came up with a different concept, completely turning the orientation. Suddenly we could see the house and how it would be, sheltered by surrounding trees, but yet with fine views. The fresh snow showed us tracks of the creatures who would share the place with us—the heart-shaped hoof marks of several deer, the single file steps of a fox, the little hand-marks of squirrels, birds feeding on weed seeds and even an otter's belly slide along an old fence line. In one of the aspens was a fresh woodpecker bore. Out on the as-yet unfrozen lake, we heard geese honking intimately to themselves. A raven flapped over, calling his mate. Then the two of them played over our valley before they parted.

Walking down to Heron Bay, as we called the nearby inlet of the lake access lot, we stared across the sparkling lake backed by snow-clad evergreens, watching a small raft of mergansers, safely distant from the far shore. Even the waves sounded cold and stiff. I would always miss the exceptional pines of Foley Mountain and the wind-song in them, but there was so much to love here too. Already I was feeling a homing sense each time I returned to the clearing where we envisioned our home.

Before we left that day, I made one more little foray. The tree-lined gully beside our property now had a stream running through it, with water overflowing from our tiny pond in the meadow. Standing by the road I could hear water music. Would we hear this from an open window in a spring to come, I wondered. I followed the gully back along a small stream of deep water running next to our property. Perhaps I could plant a few wild irises here?

Although technically we didn't own our lot yet, at the first of December, we drove over to the land for an early meeting with our friend, Terry Martin. Once our offer to purchase was accepted, we wanted Terry to install our septic system and do our groundwork. On our twenty-minute trip, we met only a single vehicle: a marked change from the ever-increasing traffic close to Westport. Just after we turned off the deserted highway, we caught sight of the startlingly white head and spread white tail of a bald eagle sailing high overhead, working powerfully, confidently with the wind.

Although a new dusting of snow made all pretty and new again, the clear cold was almost unbearable as we stood on stiff, frozen feet getting advice from Terry. But oh, the satisfaction when he approved of our choice of site. It was thrilling to stamp out a house outline in the snow. I noticed that Terry measured in strides, not steps as we did. As I used to do in childhood, I played at imagining "Here I am standing in the kitchen. Now I am in the writing room. This will be our bedroom."

Reading the ground with a practiced eye, Terry could tell where the underlying rock would be and could make educated guesses. He showed us a good way for our potential driveway to run, and before he left he praised our house site as a natural. In his experience, there were no longer many good lots such as this one available. So many places had become overbuilt, he told us, but here, he thought, the lots were surprisingly generous.

While Barry and Terry talked on, gossiping now, I kept getting glimpses of exquisite views through the now-leafless trees. Looking through the stripped-down tree silhouettes of winter, I could see that our home would feel very different with the changing of the seasons. While in summer we would be sheltered by green woods, after the leaves fell the views would open to the curving valley and the forests beyond.

After Terry drove off in his big white truck, we slipped down into the valley to see how our tiny spring-fed pond was doing. Where all the beaver ponds at the park now were hidden by thick milky lids of ice, dark, living water still welled up from this one. From here, we skirted close to the base of the dramatic, towering, forested ridge, which was now a winter landscape of stark white birches and dark green cedars. Circling back to the road again, we paused to listen to the musical stream running through the gully beside our lot. By chance we looked up to see a glistening white bird with black-tipped wings flying dreamily high overhead, drifting towards our bay. And then we saw fifteen more. Snow geese. We were beginning to feel the power of living so close to a lake.

While we waited for our new home, we began reading whatever we could find about the area where we would be living. Our friend Don Goodfellow loaned us his late mother's precious copies of Laura Lee Davidson's books celebrating Bobs Lake, *A Winter of Content* (1922) and *Isles of Eden* (1924). "I am tired to death,"

wrote Davidson. "I need rest for at least one year. I have loved the woods all my life, I long to see the year go round there just once before I die."

Reading *A Winter of Content*'s account of a solitary woman's precious year living alone on an island, I felt we were being introduced to our new home country. Imagine. Woods filled with trilliums! Since ravaging deer had overrun the park, this loveliest of spring flowers had almost disappeared. Would we find them again at our new place? After Davidson's evocative books, we were eager to know more, so we felt lucky to discover local author Lloyd B. Jones's *The Damned Lakes: An Environmental History of Crow and Bobs Lake*. This turned out to be an excellent introduction to the area, examined from the environmental angle, that which interested us most. Along with a sketch of First Nations' history, the book described timber, fishing, mining, the flooding of the lakes, the early tourists: all were included.

Back facing realities, though, there followed an unpleasant week when we saw our treasured land through others' eyes. Unfortunately, for all that the sun was radiant and the countryside was sparkling with pretty new snow, the day we showed our new place to visiting friends, the temperature was breathtakingly cold. Inevitably, being out of doors was unpleasant for these city friends who weren't dressed for the outdoors. Worse, when confronted with the solitude, which we found beautiful, they were uneasy. When it came to house advice, most of their well-meant help simply wasn't useful for us. As owners of a large home, they were unable to fathom the very different logistics of a small house where there simply were fewer design options. For us it was simple: if you took space for one room, you robbed another. And yet, for all their doubts, I still had faith that our house would have charm and be homelike, and even, I hoped, have a measure of grace.

Then, the friends who came for dinner the following Saturday night also were eager to discuss our place. From their guarded hints we gathered that neither liked the land we had chosen and that hurt. "Well, I guess it was bound to be a come down after all you've got at the park," one of them said, not looking at us.

That night I consoled myself by turning again to Laura Lee Davidson, the author who had so loved her time at Bobs Lake. She heard whip-poor-wills there in her days. Would we hear them when we moved in?

On a mild, heavily grey Friday soon afterwards, to erase the hurtfulness of our friends' dismissiveness, I headed over to the land by myself to mess around. As always, I felt happy and snug at the house site. But when I looked down into the low land, I was startled to see that this time it truly did look more like a marsh than a meadow there. Still, living intimately with a wetland would be a special thing, I thought. I made my way down through the meadow onto the cartway. By now my boots were getting soggy from the very wet snow. Never before had the valley land looked more water than grass, and this was puzzling since we had had scant precipitation lately.

Perhaps the heron pond would hold the answer. As I headed up Box Hill and into our woods I was pleased to discover several small beech trees in our part of the woods, a species we had not been able to find here before. When we were searching for a home last year, I frivolously muttered to Barry that our new place would have to include a beech tree, like the dooryard tree that I had grown up with. When we first walked here, excitedly looking at trees, I was distressed to see none of these trees on our property, for all that there were such fine ones in the area. However, for every tree lacking on our land here, we had found a new one, such as our wonderful burr oak and the superb triple ash by the pond. And now we could add this beech, flourishing in the open damp near the pond. One of the first ways we felt compelled to know our new home-to-be had been to begin a list of the species of trees on the property, and already we had discovered twenty.

How darkly green the mossy cliffs were in winter. Hearing water rushing from the direction of the grotto, I promised myself I would visit that later. But first, I fought my way through prickly ash and whiplash saplings to the pond itself. There I halted. The beaver-flooded meadow that was on our property had been completely drained, with plates of ice strewn on the shore. Before me was the sad sight of beaver channels, still filled with water. Turning towards the main pond where the heron nests were, I was shocked to discover what must have been a beaver's bank lodge, and now appeared to have had the front hacked off it with something like an axe. I could still hear water draining from the main dam, and hurried as best I could through the shrubby lowland and scrambled up onto the shore of the big pond itself. Here too the escaping water had left crazily leaning ice sheets. Now I knew that the flooding in our valley had been caused by the deliberate draining of this pond. On this heavy, damp afternoon, anxiously I clambered over onto the horseshoe-shaped dam, but I couldn't see signs of a beaver in the pond although I did spot broad otter slides on the slushy ice. Darkness was closing around me and I knew I should turn back. Even at two o'clock, the low light of the approaching winter solstice made it feel close to nightfall. But this time, when I approached the ruined lodge I spotted a mid-sized beaver briskly swimming in the pathetic, tiny remaining puddle in front of it. Seeing me, he dove in alarm.

At the park, if one pond broke, there were others. On the extremely rare occasions when a trapper intruded, Barry could use his position as park superintendent to intervene. But that afternoon, surveying the vicious destruction, it was beginning to occur to me that when we left Foley Mountain to become stewards of such a small acreage, we would be moving closer to edginess.

Shortly before Christmas, in an advance that felt both scary and exciting, we got official notification that the township plan for our "subdivision" had passed, along with a long, legal letter of conditions, which we turned over to our lawyer.

That evening, with a full moon, and a good dusting of snow everywhere, we were tempted into going to see the land by moonlight. We drove over in the exquisite cold light, looking at everything with fresh eyes. Across our bay we spotted a few house lights and it occurred to me that once we were established we could actually walk across the frozen lake at night to go visiting. When we left our car outside our own land, we entered a dream of perfect silence, perfect stillness. All that was most lovely about winter was spread around us. Tugging our scarves up about our chins, we set out under the enormously high dark dome of night with its brilliant silver disk, playing the game of following the future driveway, winding around the front island of trees. *The luster of moonlight* was searching, illuminating, exquisite. There was our house site, as always looking, and feeling, just right. On across to our trail down to the valley, the Deer Run we were calling it, and out into the wonder of the whole large but sheltered valley under the moon's radiance. We stood looking across the valley of silvery light at the powerful high ridge, a wall of evergreens limned with stark white birch limbs. Then slowly, slowly we drove back home over roads of crunching, powdery snow.

Our younger son Jeremy arrived home for the holiday, and on Christmas Day at noon we brought him over to see the site of our new home, anxiously awaiting his reaction. On another cold, cloudy day, even to us the land looked austere. As he looked at the house site as well as our favourite places, the spring-fed pond and Box Hill, Jeremy was very quiet. His pain at the thought of our leaving his childhood home was clear. But although he said little, his generous spirit seemed open to the changes ahead for his parents.

As we were leaving, we passed a house adjacent to the development where visiting grandchildren were flying downhill on toboggans, just as I had told Jeremy I hope we will do at Box Hill.

That afternoon, when Morgan and Rick arrived to join us for a party, Morgan warmed us by telling us that they had been talking about how nice it would be driving over to our place to share holidays. After Morgan and Rick went back to their own home, as they did every Christmas, Barry and Jeremy walked out to Spy Rock together to look out over the little village. On the walk, Jeremy told his father that his fiancé Karen and he had talked of bringing their future children to visit at Christmas and that he now thought our new land would be a fine place for them.

It mattered greatly to Barry and me that our family appreciated our new home. But at the same time, I was aware of how much our leaving Foley Mountain would mean to our sons. The park had been home to them from the time that Morgan was only four, while for Jeremy it was the only home he had known. In every kind of weather our boys had made their way home from where the school bus dropped them at the front gate, walking the mile-long park road and down our laneway, sometimes trudging, sometimes racing home with news. In winter they skated on the small pond beside our laneway, making trails through the scrub willows there. Then in spring they knelt on the rocks by it, scooping up tadpoles and caddisfly larvae.

I believe the times alone with nature gave them a needed peace and a chance to reflect. After school Morgan headed out to the bare rocks in front of the house, mulling over the day that had passed. When they were thirteen, Jeremy and his two best friends had homeschooled for a year. This had given them free afternoons to explore, and once they even crawled inside the chamber of a nearby forsaken beaver lodge. Heading several fields back of the house, Morgan had built himself a fine teepee. One afternoon, walking through the pines at the campground, he had the unforgettable experience of seeing coyotes pass by, close to him, blurred by heavily falling snow.

Behind the house was a spruce plantation, where the crowded trees grew to a great size. Each Christmas, the four of us and a merry assortment of dogs walked back with a toboggan to cut and fetch home a fragrant tree. One year, Jeremy even brought his high school class to choose a tree for their classroom. So many memories for them. So many memories for all of us.

And one last note. Late in the holiday Barry and I finally got around to one of our traditions, reading *The Wind in the Willows's Dulce Domum*, the beloved story of the Mole being drawn to revisit his old home. Ever since the destruction of my own childhood home in a woods in Mississauga, I had been unable to read this without tears. This year, though, sitting up in bed listening to Barry reading aloud the familiar words, I realized that while I still was sympathetic for the homesick Mole, I no longer felt sad myself.

I checked. Surely, I still felt some distress? But no. It was ended. No more. And today, perhaps more surprisingly, Barry admitted that he found the same thing happening for him. After thirty-five years of searching, he said, he thought we were going to an enduring home at last. That night I was astonished and happy to find that a change had taken place without my ever noticing it.

IV

Planning in Earnest

When Jeremy went back to university after the holiday, it was finally time to narrow the choices on our house plan. After a long, dark afternoon with papers, books, and magazines spread over my handmade log cabin quilt that covers our bed, I felt I had come very close to a design that not only would work, but would please us. Now, at last, we had enough to get a proper estimate from a builder, although I still hadn't tackled the basement layout or the positioning and number of windows.

Of all the references that helped me, the most inspiring was Christopher Alexander's *A Pattern Language*. This tome on architectural thinking helped me understand what mattered in planning our house and how to get to the heart of it.

But even before I turned to Alexander, I was aware of what a difficult task choosing locations for windows would be. As he stressed, when selected with sensitivity, the location of these made an immense difference. Unfortunately, he believed that the final placing of windows and doors could not be done on paper. It had to be done on site: a luxury that would not be available to us. In terms of his thinking, we would be at a disadvantage because we would not be able to stand with a partially built house and tell a builder that we now could see that our original choices were unsatisfactory and needed to be changed.

Of course I knew there was no way I could learn enough about architecture or even the psychology of space to proceed particularly effectively. However, it was surprising how much I could refine my thinking. For instance, I discovered that I felt better when a window was as wide as my normal field of vision, which, I found on testing it, actually was not just straight ahead, but extended half that much again on either side to accommodate peripheral vision.

The Sunday after Christmas we drove over to our house site to find out exactly what dimensions we could fit into our chosen space. First we pried up frozen rocks and made a pile to use for delineating the boundaries of our house. (Although I wanted to get started, I couldn't help appreciating some complex, unusual ones, laden with crystals, which reminded me of what a pleasure it would be to learn more about the geology of the area.) Then we measured out widths in footsteps. Finally, after much chucking of rocks to outline our space, we were satisfied that we could indeed fit a reasonable house of an affordable size-range in the perfect, but narrow site available behind a berm of rock and trees that sheltered us from the road. Without a doubt we had our home spot now.

From the house site we faintly heard the sounds of the ice lid that was thickening over the lake. Crossing the road and slithering along the ice-glazed lane, we scrambled out onto the rocky exposed beach that looks across the bay to the high ridge of the access lot. Standing together we were surrounded by the magical booming and whinnying of the freezing lake. Crunching over the frozen mud, we explored along the exposed edge of the bay, which is created when the lake is drained down into the Tay River and the Rideau Canal system for winter.

Next, we went on with our plan to explore the other sites before they were taken over by new owners, so that we would know something of our neighbouring land in case a time came when we no longer would have permission to visit these. First we walked up the long, winding driveway to a fine high vantage point, looking both away down the lake past islands, and then back towards our Heron Bay too. The lake ice was polished and glistening, and far away to the northwest we spotted a couple of ice huts, out early. From one of these we saw a distant ATV creeping over the ice, heading far south and out of sight.

Although the day was flint cold, we stopped at the sold corner lot where a road had been scraped in, and we followed that. This had been the original homestead lot, with a small barn foundation and a lilac bush. Winding and twisting, the new road ascended higher up the steep hill than I had expected, looking out over a back bay, though this view surely would be curtailed when the leaves appeared next spring.

With our growing understanding of what was needed, we played at criticizing this lot, guessing where the septic system could go and how the owners would manage a foundation where the building footprint surely was too small. Then Barry persuaded me to follow a deer-path up to the very top of the ridge, a dream of a place. We imagined having a tent there in summer, sleeping at the top of the world, where we could gaze out over bays in all directions.

Standing there, we said that buying land would be one of the most addictive acts we could ever know. Then, as we descended to the road again, we began imagining what it might be like to buy the fifty-acre lot next to this homestead one, and, of course, the lot adjacent to our own one, as well. Still, as we tramped back through the field lane to our home lot, once again, as always, we had to admit that we felt rich with the great diversity of our own twenty acres. Indeed, I was finding so much to appreciate, I told Barry that I could be happy if I could go no further than our own house clearing, with its surrounding little hills and views and interesting trees. But to also have the riches of the rocky wooded slopes behind us, the big island of trees, the tiny field pond, the meadow, the bay meadow at the back, Box Hill, the ironwood forest, the heron pond!

Early in January, we revisited the prefab homes company, spending the morning with a representative, going over house details. Although, he was clear, experienced and businesslike, and listened attentively to our plans and wishes, we were dismayed to learn that the company's house-building charges excluded the many services he called *groundwork*. Leaving the office, I felt as close to despair as I had been during the process so far. We couldn't come

close to affording his price. Only the thought of our land kept me
from tears.

The following Saturday we drove to Home Depot and spent
two hours on a fact-finding mission scrutinizing cabinets, sinks,
windows, counters, floors and much more. To our surprise we
found this experience less daunting than we had expected.
Everything was usefully laid out. The many staff were cheerful,
available and helpful. Most of all, we were able to get an idea of
what was available and of possible prices, so we could negotiate
better with builders. A few times I had intimations of how pleasing
it would be to have a bright new counter or to open windows
without a struggle.

The next morning we got up early and by nine we were seated
together at our long old farm kitchen table to draw a careful plan on
graph paper. As a child, I loved messing with houses. It began with
leaf houses, the ones where room partitions were raked clear on a
lawn, bordered by leaf walls. With an easy leap of imagination I
called out, "Let's say this is the kitchen." Or, "Supposing this is the
door." Later, I leaned precariously from the tree house my father
built, seeing the forest below from an entirely different vantage
point. Soon after that, my woodland fort had windows, and a shiny
tin mirror over the kitchen sink, and a comforting sense of shelter.

This morning, however, the charm of those early dream homes
was entirely missing. Composing a final plan proved to be
excruciating, detailed work. New points we hadn't thought of kept
springing up. Often there was the sucked-in-breath feeling of trade-
offs.

We started with the kitchen, where Barry was able to get me a
superbly useful pantry, while I insisted on a long, broad peninsula,
which would divide the dining room and kitchen. In an old kitchen
design book, which I had picked up for fifty cents, we found good
details about cabinet location and appliance footprints, and the
necessary counter space around appliances. I sacrificed a window on

the north side, but otherwise this would be a fine kitchen for me to work in. And after that, planning the dining room followed easily. Still, as we worked on, I felt more and more uneasy.

Only later in the morning did I fully understand what was troubling me. Now I was up against reality I was beginning to fear that all we would be getting was a vinyl-clad box with none of the charm or interest I'd hoped for. Like a squelched little girl, I felt my dreams were being trampled by practicality.

Over the years, some things had become part of my vocabulary of dreams. "If I ever have a house of my own I will have floor-to-ceiling windows floating over a valley, like those I saw in the Venchiarutti house long ago, decks where one can wander out into the day, as I had experienced when I stayed with friends at Wakefield, casement windows to fling open, like those in my childhood bedroom, a studio flooded with sun, an oriel window like the one I added in a novel I was writing, just for fun. As we began the hard process of firming things up, Barry, the practical one, had to keep saying a relentless "no" to every extra I suggested, while it was acutely painful for me to acknowledge that I would never have these things. Under the pressure, he snapped and I argued back.

Eventually, very late, we stopped for a brief, tense lunch, but then went right back to our task of planning a house that would last us into old age. By the time we stopped at three, we had a fairly professional plan, which mostly pleased us.

Climb the short flight of stairs and enter at the centre of our house. A hall stretches the length of the building, dividing east and west sides. Turn left and you will find yourself facing west into a light-filled kitchen, divided from the dining room by a long, wide peninsula. This is a kitchen intended for work and designed to enhance the pleasure of making big casseroles, freezing vegetables from our garden, and sharing meals with friends and family. Across from the kitchen, the living room is the place where we have combined the most requirements into one space. To give a sense of shelter and tranquility, it is separated from the hall and dining room by a half-wall, and from the hall and kitchen by the back of a large pantry. There are windows on two sides of this room. At the north end will be our woodstove, while tucked into the southern end is a sitting area, sheltered behind the full wall of the pantry. If you then walk back south along the long central hall, you pass a small guest bedroom and a larger bedroom for Barry and me with long, low-silled windows facing east and south. Across the way is my writing room-to-be, with two windows, and also the bathroom. All of this is a tremendous amount to fit into the limitations of such a small space.

I came away thinking that we had designed a plan that would really work for us but which would make us happy too. If we had lost features, we also had gained some. For instance, I now could envision sitting in a dining room where we would have fine views in three directions. There were practical details that worked well too. We realized how easy any deliveries would be because we would be able to pull up a truck directly to the walk-out basement. For some years I had held onto a pile of handsome cedar panelling, which came from the home where I grew up and was originally a gift from my carpenter grandfather. I had the gratifying thought that we could use this for the half-wall that would separate our living room from the dining room. Now that we were done, we felt proud of ourselves for accomplishing our plan. Already we had made far more decisions than I would have expected to have finished at this point. The tricky planning of kitchen cabinets and window sizes was done. We even had a rudimentary materials list. Now, if only we could get an estimate we could live with.

The snow fell each day now and we were locked in with bitter cold. We made a plan to order seedling trees for our place. After all these years of living on a rented property, to be able to think of planting trees in terms of our own land felt touching and exciting. We also made an appointment to meet with a young local builder who came well recommended.

One morning Barry stumbled sleepily down to breakfast. "What will we call our place," he asked. "It should have a name. What about *Snipe Vale*," he said facetiously.

I thought a few moments as I buttered toast. "Or maybe *Meadow Sweet* or *Still Point*," I offered. He beamed with the soft radiance of love for our new home. "*Meadow Sweet*, I think," he told me, thought a moment more and then asked, "What about *Still Point Meadow*?"

As I washed our few dishes and set out bread to rise in the big yellow gripstand bowl, covering it with one of my hand-woven towels, I still was thinking about the name. What I remembered most was the vibrant meadow at the very heart of our new home place. No matter what the season, it always felt alive. I turned to Barry, and it was no longer a question: "*Singing Meadow*," I said. It was not just the resounding song of hundreds of frogs in spring, nor the call of crickets in late summer, nor even the music of the many field birds who also saw our land as home. There was something about this bowl of a valley, threaded with water, and wavering with tall grass, which was singing always.

"That's it," he responded immediately. "We've got it."

Despite the tension, this was a touching interlude of commitment and hope. During the process it had occurred to me that although this difficult and long-lasting negotiating might break us, instead it might force us to hone our negotiating and relational skills as a couple. We were relearning how to articulate clearly, to identify what mattered and how to achieve as much as we could while respecting the other, to learn to back off, be patient, compromise. Sometimes I wondered whether this would be a refresher course that would help us for the rest of our days.

The next week we took our new plans and met with the local builder. While drumming his fingers on the shiny finish of the fancy picnic table in his office, he pointed out that he would have to charge the same fee for our unfinished basement as for the upper storey, in other words double what we had been quoted by others.

Then he finished by showing us pictures of the impressive home he was working on. We came home crestfallen and consoled ourselves by grabbing up Molly, our tiny, curmudgeonly old dachshund, and driving over to the land, ostensibly to check where the winter sun would fall at three pm. Would it flood into the dining room as we wanted it to?

Soon after that, a young man came to see Barry about volunteering at the park. He had heard that Barry's job would soon be available, and he wanted to see the house because he also was interested in applying for the job. Although it was encouraging to think of such a likeable and committed person living in our home, this visit made leaving Foley Mountain feel very real. Describing all the good things about being there, such as no commuting time to get to work, the friendliness of the community, not to mention the many off-trail rocky ridges and distant ponds where no one else ever went, I felt a cold shadow hover over me.

At one moment, imagining planting a new tree or vine at our new place, or thinking how happy we would be with our new home, I would have a glimpse of delight. And then, thinking of leaving a place so rich with memories, my heart would feel torn again.

At the end of January, we went over to the land again. "I miss it," Barry agreed when I suggested going. We parked and walked out to the end of the point along a snowmobile trail. It was the first warmish day in weeks, and everything over at our land looked infinitely beautiful. I was beginning to be familiar with the trees — the immense red oak at the head of the bay, some fine beeches high over the road, the two twisted ashes guarding the end of the point. In the bright afternoon light, exquisite bluish cloud shadows were creeping over the snow-clad bay that was dotted with ice huts. Looking far, far down the lake, we could see island after island.

There was definitely a February-ish look to the landscape now. The trees felt as if they too were tingling with intimations of spring. Down the lake we heard ravens rauking.

I was surprised to find that I liked the idea that we were in with others on building a new community here. I wanted to discover who the other people would be, and hoped to work together with them as a community. At this stage, I looked forward to seeing people settle the place, though perhaps when it all was built up, I wouldn't.

After our walk we went to our own place. As always we noticed the alluring glint of view behind the front line of trees. We snowshoed up what would be our driveway and puttered, looking at the house site for a few minutes, prattling about gardens and hose lengths, and wandered down through the light, deep snow, glancing across the valley, acknowledging our burr oak, our marker tree.

We were getting very anxious to go up onto the ridge and also to explore the fifty acres for sale up there as soon as the deep, heavy snow shrank. But for now, we went to our tiny pond, with its spring still gently flowing in the depth of what was an exceptionally cold winter. Then we plodded back up the Deer Run and happily out to the car. Before leaving, though, we slipped down the boat launch road, seeing where the cottagers who lived there had visited, having a winter holiday with a skating rink cleared on the ice and a Santa Claus outside.

Although I was glad to discover four older shaggy yellow birches down near the lake, I was sorry that so far we hadn't been able to find them elsewhere in the development. The gleaming, curly-barked trees were among my favourites at the park. So far, here, we had found American and blue beech, sugar maples, red, white and burr oaks, bitternut hickory, ash, ironwood, elm, basswood, and several kinds of aspens.

But back home at the park, both Barry and I had been floundering through this anxious waiting while time was spilling away. With no plan of an affordable builder, I no longer wanted to think about the trees that we had ordered to plant this spring.

On the one hand, this was the lovely heart of winter, with fluffy passing clouds and blue snow shadows and deer and wild turkeys who came to our park house front door and hosts of little birds, including, surprisingly, robins, but always there was a knot in my stomach. The house-building dilemma was beginning to feel as if it was beyond our ability to resolve.

Finally, on the advice of our friend David Pollard, Barry phoned Paul Musselman, a Portland builder David worked with, and they talked for the best part of an hour. This time, when he came to report to me, he was hopeful. Earlier we had heard that Paul only worked on renovations and did not build complete houses. But when Barry asked him outright whether our house would be worth his while, to our delight he said he would consider the project and asked us to leave our plans with him. He was already fully booked for the year ahead, but thought he might want to work for us the following one. Having Paul build our house for us would mean that technically Barry and I would act as site supervisors, with at least some responsibility for arranging with the tradespeople and suppliers. But if we could work out a deal with Paul, having to take on this extra responsibility would be worth it.

While we waited for Paul's answer, we grabbed the chance of an extremely rare mild day to go walking on the land. Although we tossed around the idea of exploring new regions, something we really wanted to do while the lake was frozen and the packed-down snowmobile trails made walking easy, once again we were drawn to walk the old cartway through our back field in a moving and dreamlike way. Each stop along the way felt precious and full of interest, so it was a lingering, gazing-around sort of walk.

But all the same, because we had been closed in by snow for too long now, we were impatient to get off the trails. Today at last the walking over the wind-packed snow was easy. First, we clambered up to look out from the summit of Box Hill and try to imagine what our one small, New England-style stone wall would look like without a blanket of snow. And of course, after the December damage, we were anxious to assure ourselves that there was no further damage to the beaver lodge in the heron pond. Now that all was heavily blanketed in snow, the earlier violence was muted, and we found no further evidence of the trapper who had hacked open the beaver lodge.

On and on we went, stepping through an old opening in a rail fence onto further fields and hills so alluring that we circled on until we ended down in the valley where woodpeckers already had started drumming their spring calls. Otherwise, the winter silence was profound. There was more porcupine evidence than we would have liked, but the only sign of deer was a small wandering trail threading up into our land and a bigger one at the fence rails, where we also met a small flock of chickadees.

With the coming of March, I was focusing on the newly arriving wonders of spring while I waited for Paul to give us his estimate. I also was mentally fingering certain small dreams. A friend had loaned us her copy of Sara Susanka's popular design book, *The Not so Big House*. In spite of the promising title, much of this was designed for far grander houses than the one we had planned. Certainly, if we had been able to afford them, the beautiful woods used, the charming, interesting windows, and the quirky, inventive architecture would have been our ideals. All the same, seeing these inspiring houses did give me ideas. For example, the gorgeous rugs made me think of how much textiles could add to a home's feeling of theatre. As a weaver, I knew I would be able to contribute some of these. Looking at the book I felt inspired, sure my home vision was right. Maybe we could salvage enough to make the box feel more like a place that would express us.

Although I was eager to start planting there, legally we didn't even own this land yet, so, very reluctantly I decided not to order plants that year. For the same reason we were resisting cutting out scrub and dead wood to open views, although I would have liked to get ahead with this.

Meanwhile, spring was creeping in slowly. When we went to walk along the cartway at Singing Meadow, we held our coats open to the new and welcome warmth. As always, we were looking and looking, and yet never able to take it all in. In the softening snow walking was heavy going, but always there was that feeling of gazing in wonderment at the dazzling bowl of the valley. Eventually, we took off our coats and plunked down on them under the spreading triple ash by our little pond, shaping the snow beneath us to fit our forms like chairs. From here we gazed down at the widening patches of opening water on our little pond, while Barry tossed snowballs to plop into the dark water.

As we waited for Paul to arrange a meeting, I was finding the uncertainty nearly unbearable. I no longer could write; in fact, every step I took was an effort. In an attempt to turn away from misery and anxiety I bought a small red and green Amish wall quilt kit with beautiful feathers and hearts to quilt and I stitched faithfully on it, making it a present for my new house-to-be. The acorn door knocker sat waiting on the bookshelf at the foot of the stairs, where I passed it many times a day, sometimes looking at it with affection and sometimes stroking its satisfying roundness.

On a Sunday late in March, I awoke early with a rush of urgent need to go to the land. Unfortunately, instead of the promised sun, there was a dank, gloomy mist in keeping with the anxiety that lurked in the back of our minds. Slowly I worked through my yoga practice, and as I moved into poses with as much care as I could muster, I glanced to the west. To my delight, big rents were tearing open in the sky, exposing a wonderful blue and turning the heavy cloud to fleecy, flying puffs.

Right after lunch we hurried over to Singing Meadow. At the forest-shaded park there hadn't been much sense of a spring run-off of water yet, but elsewhere it was different. On the road, as we were driving over, we saw flooded pastures and rushing brooks. All was sparkle and rush with a feeling of the land being cleansed and renewed. In a farm stream I was elated to see a heron, the first one I had seen that year.

As we sloshed through puddles along the road to the point, I said to Barry "This is one of those rare times that will never come again. Our relationship with the land here will never be this pure again. Every detail here is poignant and precious and still new to us."

Now that they were becoming exposed, I was relishing all the diversity of soils: the gritty sand of the peninsula, the red, slick clay at our road frontage, the blue clay of the pond, and even the powdery dubious soil where our house excavation would be. All along the peninsula road I considered the access land, which we owned in common with a number of other lot-owners here, finding a pine under which I could stand to hear the wind, as I did back at the park, a couple of sitting spots with choice views over Heron Bay, and even a small, low place where it would be fairly easy to get down to the water. Along the way, we discovered evidence of a rampaging beaver who apparently had clambered all the way up the steep hill from the lake to wreak his destruction on a large maple. Passing the immense guardian ash trees, we strode down to the tip, looking out across the frozen bay past the wealth of islands. On the way back we stopped to appreciate the afternoon light dappling a superb spreading beech, and looked wistfully at one cottage of natural board and batten, with skylights, a spreading verandah, and sheltering trees. How comfortable we could be living full-time in what was only someone else's summer place. Looking down off the high peninsula, we noticed a long river of water thrusting a channel through the bay ice, a river that we now knew came from our own pond and grotto by way of the little stream in the gully next to our land.

Back at our own lot, the snow hadn't yet vanished. To get in to our land, we had to wrestle through drifts of knee-high snow, but how good it felt to be able to walk about and visit our house site. And, oh, how wonderful. The valley had become a water meadow again, or a *silver meadow* as author Robert Michael Pyle called such a place, shining and radiant. Every day of my life I appreciated more the preciousness of water. *Holme*, Pyle wrote, was the Old Norse term for these winter-flooding fields, and in a sense I knew that of all the places on our land, this everchanging meadow, now singing with flowing waters, would most truly be my home.

We explored The Glade, the wooded point just behind where we envisioned having our living room. There were so many good places to sit that we would need at least six benches, I told Barry impulsively. Couldn't we just carry chairs, he asked, reasonably. But I like to prowl, hands free, and sit impromptu, and there were so many fine views that it was hard to choose where to be looking. With some difficulty, we sloshed through watery snow to visit the pond, surrounded by the musical spring run-off. Drawn to the leaping "eye" in the worn bowl of rock where the water bursts up from under the hill, we knelt, draggling our fingers against the force of the glassy, endless welling-up of cold, living water. We cupped it in our hands. Away from us it rushed out into the swollen pond, spilling over and racing across the meadow and on to the lake, and to the Tay River, and to the Rideau Canal system, and then on to the mighty St. Lawrence River and out to the sea. I took off my socks and sat with my bare feet touching the sun-warmed bare rock for a long while, watching and listening. Before we left, we clambered up to the basswoods on Box Hill, where the snow was melted, and sat listening to the stream rushing through the gully. Barry made a plan to place a few rocks in this stream so that the flow would stay musical. In this time of discovery, there was so much a feeling of the two of us being children, playing joyously.

Finally, at the end of March came the momentous day arranged for our meeting with Paul Musselman. The builder led us into his big farm kitchen, sat us down and offered us coffee and perfect orange biscotti he had made himself. The Musselmans' beautiful calico cat wandered in to see if we needed her. Then Paul gravely pulled printed estimates from his orderly folders and passed them to us.

Feeling a swell of hopefulness, I studied all the figures he had meticulously listed out and then the two of us took turns, one talking to Paul, while the other worked through our lists of necessities to compare with the estimate. Although it was a heavy, rainy morning, I felt as if the sun was coming out. When Paul stepped out to copy some pages for us, Barry looked at me intensely. "I think we can just do it."

"I feel hopeful now," I told Paul when he returned. And when Barry arrived at and circled a final amount, which we could just barely afford, I was swept by rushes of relief. What we would have was a twelve hundred square foot house, and because we had managed to fit my writing room upstairs, we would have more useful space downstairs.

"What do you think of our plan?" Barry asked Paul. "Will it work? Can you suggest any improvements?" Taking another quick look at it, Paul offered, "When the structure is up, it will be easy enough to tape the floors or even to hold up walls and move them until it feels right." I had a vision of a moveable house. I always longed to build a house, and now I would be. I wouldn't want to miss a minute of this. "When the walls are up you'll be surprised that it appears bigger than you thought," Paul murmured thoughtfully, more to himself than to us, "And then, when the interior partitions are up, you'll be worried because it seems small, and then, when the wallboard is up it will feel big again." As we talked it over, Paul observed that there often were hardware sales and he offered to store things for us if we wanted to buy them ahead. As we finished our talk, his wife Violette joined us, sharing our enthusiasm. "We came that close to having to walk away, if it hadn't been for you," Barry exclaimed. "That close."

Driving home in the rain, we were giddy, although still half-disbelieving our good fortune. As soon as we got home we phoned our sons to share our happiness, and then, with the rain stopped, and a watery sun trying to show, after lunch we drove over to the land to tell it we would be living there.

Back through fields, bare of snow at last, hand in hand we wandered, sharing our bliss. At the house site I looked in delight at what now really would be the living room, our bedroom, and the writing room. Then we prowled down the deer trail and back to the cartway, where the underground stream was still roiling out of our small pond. "Let's go back and see the heron pond." And so, on this unforgettable day, for the first time since the deep snow had receded and the ice had rotted, we did, talking ecstatically about clipping trails, looking with pleasure at the fattening tree buds of red-fisted maples and the sulphur yellow buds of the bitternut hickories. And oh, when we reached this large bowl-like pond, sheltered by steep, rocky walls, a dozen herons were flying softly, making talk I had never heard before from a heron, weaving amongst their nests. They were reclaiming their summer home. Now that we knew they had returned, we would try not to disturb these great, private birds by coming back again until after their babies were fledged, but what a wonderful, wonderful sight. As well, seeing the many chewed saplings in the wetland below the old dam, we finally had assurance that, miraculously, after the destruction of his lodge, a beaver still was living in this pond. Here, as the season progressed, I imagined finding the first marsh marigolds and then, later, cardinal flowers.

Back at the house site, I looked down the road to the alluring little hills and the protective massed white cedars, and north over to the gully with its tall maples. Coming from the water meadow below, a full-fledged creek was rushing there now. Behind the house site, our north-facing field was one of the last places still with snow. "It will be nice and shady in summer," Barry pointed out.

Home again at the park, breathless with relief, we felt our shoulders lightening. Paul offering to build us an affordable house had given us back our lives. Now I actually was glad to have a year here to be tranquil and establish myself before the havoc and excitement of building and moving. Having made peace with waiting, I was going to enjoy every bit of the time ahead. Barry called his best friend, Umberto, who told him, "That's fantastic. From now on it's all forward." From now on we would have an end in sight. We would be working towards something, instead of floundering through too many possibilities.

Now Barry and I were sustained in everything we did by a private joy, thinking of our new land and the home we would make there. Evenings I riffled happily through the Golden Bough tree nursery catalogue, considering the possibility of chestnuts and magnolias. Before long, after errands in Perth, we decided to slip over to our land by the different road we would be using now. Our stated purpose was to see whether the promised hydro lines were being installed yet. With increasing excitement, we drove past the farm country and the small brick church at DeWitt's Corners, after which the landscape became wilder and hillier. Down what would be our own road we drove, passing the big beeches on the hill, which were lit with golden spring sun. We rounded the last corner, and, oh, the ice was almost gone from the bay there. Could I have forgotten just how exciting it was to see the lakes free and alive again after the winter ice?

Sure enough, a few hydro poles had been erected. In fact, near our place, on our side of the road, was a pile of poles. How funny to be watching a community being created, rather than evolving over years. It mattered to see each step of the process. "We won't stop," Barry had cautioned me on the drive over, "Just check, that's all." Because his busy spring season was approaching, he needed to get back to work at the park. Yet it was he who had his car door open first. And immediately we were overwhelmed by a resounding shrill of peepers, calling with a loudness we'd never heard before. Our water meadow was alive with them.

In the day's surprising heat we wandered up what, in another year, would be our driveway. "We won't go beyond the site," cautioned Barry. But all the same we did, gazing and gazing at the early spring green landscape, dizzied by the peepers. A pair of mallards who were resting in our water meadow flew up protesting, and this disturbance was our sign to return to the car. But I was finding that every time I had to leave Singing Meadow, I caught myself thinking that I could happily stay there forever. This was a place where I could rest my heart.

Good Friday came late that year. On a soft, grey day filled with many arriving migrants, we finally were able to explore the high ridge that guards our valley. First we had to thrust our way through a dense protective wall of white cedars that ascended the ridge. Hauling ourselves up the steep hill beyond that, we discovered a sheltered, hidden woodland of tall old maples and fine spreading beeches, growing from a ledge of almost park-like grassy understorey. Above this we came upon a fascinating tableland, strewn with glacial boulders, and with only a few stunted bonsai-like trees. Meandering along the rim of this plateau, we reached a westward-facing rocky outcropping where we could scan over a vast distance beyond the many bays of the lake. A gull skimmed over us, the first of the year, speaking of summer coming and cottage jollity. Below us three newly returned turkey vultures sailed past, capturing the warming thermals rising from the valley far below us. Over the valley, a merlin trembled its wings, hovering.

When finally we reluctantly left the lonely tableland, carefully skirting the heron pond to avoid disturbing the splendid, gangly birds, we caught a charming glimpse of one with its long beak hanging over its stick nest. And then we ended this long, adventurous walk sitting together on the bleached pressed grass at the top of Box Hill, looking over our realm. In the distance, we heard a loon. Very, very exciting.

Unable to stay away, on the very late Easter Sunday, a day of surprising heavy heat inserted into lingering winter, we returned to Singing Meadow. Although the lake itself still had a translucent lid of rotting ice, some of the bays were open and dancing again. Before we began the chores we had come for, we walked over to the shore, where there now was a stretch of beautiful blue-black open water alive with whitecaps and tingly broken ice. Then we returned to make a start on clearing out some of the debris in the woods encircling our house site, hoping to make it a pleasant, easy place to walk. It felt good to me to be working on what would be our own place. This clearing of the woodlands ran deep in me. It came from watching my father wrenching and snapping and hauling, making piles that were safe havens for creatures, and, in his opinion, making the woods of my childhood a better place. Since then I had learned that the forest detritus was a necessary part of the forest process, and besides I had neither the time nor the wish to tidy everywhere. But although my aim that day was merely to open walking places, I found that I could hardly help the impulse to clear.

So warm was the morning that I actually became hot and sweaty. Molly, our tiny dachshund, wandered exploring zealously, her mahogany-red fur glistening in the June-like heat. Finally she lay down in a shady, leafy nest, and, because she was always unreasonably afraid I would leave her behind, she was watching me anxiously. At noon we took our picnic lunch and our collapsible chairs and sat gazing down the valley, dazed and tranquil in the midday warmth. Herons were flying steadily back and forth from the lake to their nesting pond. Woodpeckers were drumming in our woods. A kingfisher flashed past, scolding. Overpowered by all there was to see, I finally let my eyelids close. Later, feeling a gaze on me, I glanced up to see a bald eagle powerfully flapping down the valley to the lake, moving more smoothly than in winter when his strokes were storm-buffeted. In the beating sun, his white head glistened.

To celebrate the wonderful day and Easter, we finished by taking a small fork off the main road. This old farm road appeared unchanged since the days before the Second World War. Bordered by snake fences, it ran through a cedar swamp and up a hill where it became a cottage road. The cottages here were all unobtrusive, and spoke of the pleasures of summer and happy times.

There was an incredulous happiness to our visits to the land as April ended. The following weekend we worked faithfully over there all day Saturday and Sunday morning as well. But before we set out on the second day, I phoned our friend Hedy, who now would be a close neighbour, and asked her if she'd like to meet us later on for tea. We brought our folding chairs, and made thermoses of tea to have along with ginger biscuits.

For fun, I took bulbs I had saved from a pot of forced daffodils and planted them on the little rise by the gully. Our official business was to get a sense of where the baby trees we had ordered should go when they were delivered the following week, and we had a happy time planning this, but we also seized an afternoon while spring was approaching and wandered freely, letting love of the land fall down around us like rain in this sweet time. There was always so much of interest that we didn't move very quickly. It looked as if the climate of our new area might be a week behind that of our present home. We were pleased to spot the very first mottled dogtoothed violet leaves, and later I discovered shoots of a tiny bloodroot. We ended by walking up Box Hill to touch the sky.

After that we just had time to set up for our first guest when Hedy and her German shepherd, Sage, rolled up in Hedy's jaunty red Tracker. Sage looked right at home, prowling, fleet and low-slung, ranging widely, circling back to encourage our Molly, who was so much smaller. Although Hedy's walking was disturbingly difficult, she insisted on being shown things, and was encouragingly enthusiastic. "Don't you just want to stay here?" she exclaimed, and of course we did. I was mildly shocked at my disloyalty to the park, where I still walked appreciatively, but I felt surprisingly free here, away from the obligations of the job, and I longed to put down roots. In spirit, I told her, I was living there already.

There followed a most welcome tea, with Sage and Molly sharing ginger biscuits. We watched a pair of ospreys sailing along the valley, going to rattle the herons, as Barry said. We didn't leave until after five, taking Hedy to see the lake views down the road and gesturing to point out the craggy beeches, since she too loved beeches. I came home feeling like a cat very much stroked the right way.

Then, for the second time in a week I had the pleasure of introducing our new place to an appreciative friend. Wednesday morning I met my Scottish neighbour, Elizabeth, searching for her little white dogs, Bubble and Squeak, who had taken advantage of a radiant spring morning to go walkabout. After the wicked pair were found, I asked her if she would like to visit the land, and to my happy surprise she accepted with alacrity. Sometimes, caught between awe at the loveliness of the land and delight at being with a friend who was so attuned to everything I care for, I felt I was looking far, far back in time. I drove us down the point, where Elizabeth was very alive to the two immense "ash trees at the end of the world," as we'd taken to calling them, and was as charmed as I by the sparkle and smack of the lake water. We stopped on the way back to appreciate the fine roadside beech trees. When I observed how the trees seemed glowing with life this time of year, she knew right away what I meant. In fact, there hardly was a need for words. When we visited our lot, slowly walking all the special places, she told me that what we had was far more than she had expected, and that she could see how this was a place that would grow more precious, reveal more, with each year. For all she was older than me, she walked lightly, blithely. She was as pleased by the water welling up at our pond as we were.

Every time I went to our land I found something new to appreciate. Today, as Elizabeth and I looked about we discovered more and more tiny fragile bloodroot blossoms as well as masses of reflexed, yellow troutlily flowers, which were tucked in the rocky bit of forest behind the house site. Back in the wetland, the mallard pair, who by now were nesting, were modest and dignified, holding their ground.

When we reached the back of our land, Elizabeth pleased me by wanting to go up into the woods. Twice, once as we walked across the meadow, and once in the car on the journey home, she impetuously said a surprising thing. She said it prophetically: "I think your best writing is ahead of you. I think your best writing is yet to come, and it is here that you will do it." Nothing could have meant more to me. It was a surprising time that I shall always treasure. Her gift of appreciation of our new homeland was particularly touching because she was clearly grieved at the thought of me moving. Little murmurs escaped her like, "This will be your last Christmas at Foley Mountain." This was something I too dreaded and had been postponing contemplating.

I could see now that my friends had fallen into two camps, those who were patronizing and dismissive, for reasons I've given up trying to understand, and those like Hedy and Elizabeth, who were able to be more generously sympathetic and responsive than I could have imagined.

Tree planting day came, and I was so excited at the prospect that I didn't sleep well, but the euphoria carried me along. It turned out to be the finest of days, with bright sun and a fresh, cool wind. We were up early to drive over to the Bedford Hall where we picked up our bundle of baby trees and added it to a garbage bag with exciting-looking red dogwood shoots sticking out. These would join two spireas I'd bought on sale and an impulsive purchase, a

Wayfaring tree, which I had bought last year and planted in a spot close to the house site, where I could watch over it. On the drive along a beautiful back road, we discovered masses of delicate Dutchman's Breeches foaming out of rocky, sunlit clefts. Part way through the most secluded section of the road, it occurred to me that it was just possible that I could ride a bicycle along the dirt road there. Certainly, even if we weren't up to much of a drive later in our lives, we could go along there and find much to delight in.

Once at the land, we began sorting trees, which was not as easy as we'd expected. Since at this stage they were just short sticks with a few tight buds, we couldn't tell a Norway spruce from a white spruce.

Planting the wetland cranberries and dogwood first, we found out that in the water meadow even what appeared to be simply field was actually utterly wet. Barry would thrust in his shovel with a squishy sound and water would rush to fill the hole. That morning we could almost feel our saplings' dried roots rejoicing in the soupy blue clay bottom land, although I did wonder how they would adapt over time. The dogwood whips were a surprising two feet tall, and by the time we finished with these we were impressed to see an actual corridor of red saplings edging the wetland. Tucking in each baby tree, thinking how it would grow to become part of the landscape was deeply touching for both of us.

As we moved along with the day, I discovered that planning was a continuing difficulty. Barry wanted everything in straight lines while I preferred groves and clusters, but as long as I could think sufficiently ahead and tell Barry what I wanted, he willingly did the hard digging. After the wetland trees, we moved to the fringe of the meadow, where we planted red oaks in places where we could easily see them. Because we weren't sure about the preferences of some of the trees, we hedged our bets, trying some in different locations, snugging the handfuls of little trees in here and there.

From this we went on to the pungent-smelling infant evergreens. Across the front of our property, we made a staggered, double-line hedge of spruce, stopping to admire our extremely tall new hydro pole as we went, and then carried the line across the orchard meadow and down our side property boundary too. Along the way, we tried a few pines here and there, envisioning focal points, and we even planted a small stand of larch against the gully and our other property line. With only a few cuts of the shovel, we were changing our landscape in ways we could not even imagine, making windbreaks and shelter belts, where we hoped the area's creatures would thrive as well.

By noon we were very hungry. We crouched at the flowing stream, and dangled our hands in among the green frogs and waving grass, scrubbing the clay off enough to be able to eat decently. I had packed a fairly elaborate picnic of stuffed eggs, rye sandwiches with summer sausage, Orangina in stubby glass bottles, pickles, and tomatoes, which we ate in our camp chairs, strategically positioned out of the wind. Afterwards, we lay for a few minutes, soaking up sun, appreciating the silence. In the whole day only two cars passed by.

After lunch we hauled the bags of trees past the pond to the hills. On a whim, Barry suggested we plant three larches near the burr oak, and so we did. Nearby we admired the reflexed, chrome yellow of the trout lilies with their rust anthers, and the profusion of scattered milk-white bloodroot blossoms. By now our energy was definitely waning. It was harder to be careful about setting the trees properly erect and protecting their roots. But as we scrambled up the rocks to put more pines at the edge of the orchard meadow, I was charmed to discover a bellwort, with its shapely yellow blossoms not yet unfurled, a very few early white trilliums, and also meadow rue and red and yellow columbine.

Finally we straggled down to our sitting place at the edge of the water meadow and put in a few last trees, including the last cluster of larches. After I washed my hands, I simply sat by the stream, thankful both to be there and to be done. Making and filling one hundred and sixty holes was not easy. But all the same, this digging and plunging of hands into so many different kinds of soil, this mingling of hands among existing tree roots, this setting and nesting of tiny trees had been the best way to get to know the land itself.

Question: I knew the oaks would not grow significantly in our lifetime, but could they bear acorns? What I did know was that, with all our work and walks and love, we were making this land, in all its wealth of diversity, come alive for us.

Barry was worrying, reasonably, that we were going over to our new land too often, to the detriment of work back at the park. I tried to explain, saying that for me this was a precious time, a time when it felt necessary to keep being there over and over again, making our presence there real. Our experience of our land would never be like this again, and I wanted to savour every moment I could. Of course, I knew I also needed to respect his insistence that it would be time enough to work when we were living over there for good.

Unfortunately, this spring at the park was particularly choice. Amazing quantities of delicate pink Spring Beauty carpeted the rocks on the trail overlooking the Little Rideau Lake. At our feeders there, possibly because of the cold wetness of so many days, we had never had so many birds. There were two pair of rose-breasted grosbeaks, several towhees, both white-crowned and white-throated sparrows, many other visiting sparrows, purple finches, gold finches, and blue jays, and occasionally the cardinal and a few very tame chickadees, as well as downy and hairy woodpeckers and now two male hummingbirds, who so far had effected a neutrality. For the first time ever, the year before we would be leaving, the pear tree that I had planted twenty years ago was snowy with white bloom.

After a two-week hiatus, we slipped over to our land to see what wildflowers we could find blooming there. When we arrived, the sun broke briefly through heavy cloud, but soon afterwards the clouds re-gathered, draining the sky's colour once again. But over at the development there was not a soul. And, most wonderfully, we were greeted by the insistent, summery calls of a newly returned, very orange male oriole, who was flitting in the highest tops of the aspens, and who was answered by a more distant one down in the valley.

A green fire lay over the beautiful fields. It turned out that our own aspens were mainly large-toothed trees that didn't make much display in their leafing out, but down in the valley was a fine stand of chartreuse trembling ones. Besides the oriole, the big treat was discovering masses of small, snowy white trilliums opening out everywhere. It was noon and a new wave of birds had returned, so there was a smattering of song everywhere, plus the oriole's darting presence high overhead, but to me there was a tinge of sadness in thinking of starting again to draw birds and flowers to us at this late stage. How many years would it be at our new home before we could attract anything like the variety we had at the park?

All along we planned to visit the land on the May holiday weekend, envisioning it as a time to move trees and plants over, but also for the fun of having a holiday picnic there. However, I also wanted to go once at twilight to find whether there were thrushes and whip-poor-wills in the valley, as there surely must be. On our way, cutting across the Parrish Road, we met up with Danny Lewis at the front of his farm, and stopped to talk. He was returning with his son from a successful spring fishing trip. Yes, he knew well the farm where our land was, had cut hay there before and might do it for us. He spoke with affection of the springs there and of drinking from their cold water, knowing they never froze up.

In the brief time since we last visited, we found that the leaves had blossomed wonderfully. Everywhere there was the beauty of new white aspen leaves, the new spreading of big maples. How fine the gully looked now the trees had closed in around it. The scene over there was more like an English pastoral landscape than ever, we thought. Because we had lingered talking with Danny, by the time we arrived the light was quite low. Enchanted by hearing the music of different kinds of thrushes, coming from all over the land,

Barry burst ahead, while I paused for a moment. At my feet there were purple violets everywhere. Imagine owning a hill of violets! Gradually our pace slowed as we took in the new leafiness and the changed field vistas this brought and, best of all, the songs of many thrushes. Then, not wanting to leave, we wandered down the road, listening to the still-flowing music of the gully stream as it headed for the lake. In the distance we could hear cheery children's voices at cottages, and explosions from a few early firecrackers.

On the drive home in the dusk, Barry pointed out that I had lived at the house in the park for thirty years, which was longer than I did in my childhood home. I couldn't help thinking of what my years there had meant to me. Although it was sometimes a harsh environment, when I thought of Foley Mountain, I thought of it as a place generally dedicated to safety. I thought of the deer lying down to rest in front of our bedroom window, barely afraid of us.

How would I leave behind the two fine vegetable gardens and the long border of delphiniums and poppies, laced together with my choice antique roses? Slowly, slowly these had evolved through our own work and affection, but also with lucky finds and gifts from many. There were the things from my childhood, such as my grandmothers' plants. There was the pretty, pink-flowered bleeding heart, given to me by my one grandmother when I was four, and from my other grandmother's home in Lorne Park there was the pulmonaria, with silver-spotted leaves and flowers that magically bloomed in four colours.

But there were also wild red and yellow columbines my father had brought me when we moved to the park, and which self-seeded ever afterwards. As well there were crimson oriental poppies and tall deep blue delphiniums, which I grew from seed. When my mother saw these she said, "Granddaddy used to have great success with these," and ever afterwards I always thought of a link between us. In my border there were crimson, white, and pink peonies, like the opulent ones in my artist mother's paintings, orange tiger lilies,

which also featured in one of her glowing pictures, scented yellow
June daylilies, which my parents called lemon lilies, and the
carmine-coloured rose campion, a settlers' plant, which grew beside
our stairs when I was a child. But there were also treasures snapped
up at garden sales, plants offered by old ladies, no longer alive, like
the fat succulent hens and chickens, which I grew partly because of
their name.

Friends, family were everywhere in my gardens. When I
moved, somehow I was going to have to find a way to bring these
plants with me. Of course there were also many things I simply
loved for their own sakes, such as a large, bearded iris the colour of
the palest grey-blue sky. In my new garden there certainly would
have to be scarlet monarda for the hummingbirds who surely would
come.

But the roses would have to be left behind. For me, one of the
high points in my growing adventures had come after a winter
when I read Vita Sackville-West and caught her love for what were
called the antique ones, their history, their exceptional perfume,
their interesting forms. That spring I got an import permit and
brought in a few from a California grower of rare roses, Reine des
Violettes, a black-crimson one with dainty small petals, a magenta
and cream striped cabbage one, a shell-pink Maiden's Blush. As
these grew and prospered, I was enchanted by the glamour of their
associations, everything from Sackville-West's exceptional gardens
at Sissinghurst Castle, to the French Empress Josephine, and even
back to the Crusades and the War of Roses. Although these bloomed
only once a year, for me their beauty and fragrance surpassed the
more common ones.

Would I ever have the energy, the vision to create anew at this
stage of my life? In my new place I surely would be working with a
shorter time frame, too. Previously I had been in the habit of buying
small plants, trusting that I could grow these into larger specimens
over the years. Of course I would go on doing this, and in some
cases, as with the small trees we had planted, I accepted easily that I
would never see them mature. After all, if I never did anything here,
just loved the land as it was, that would be more than I had any

right to wish for. Wherever I looked at Singing Meadow there was so much power that it took my breath away. So yes, of course, as I saw all the overgrown but beloved perennials in my gardens at the park, I longed more than ever to start establishing things over at our new place. But it was too soon. Just wait, I said to myself.

The next week, I drove over on my own at noon. As I set out to walk the cartway, I was distracted by the eerie beauty of the shifting weather. A storm was predicted by evening. Everywhere the orange flashing orioles were shouting from treetops. I let my eyes run across the valley. Each day the landscape was moving swiftly towards the handsome woods and grasslands of high summer. Down on the flat land, as I made my way towards the pond, the heat was oppressive, yet still I rejoiced in the kind of intimately entwined walking and thinking which is only possible at the far edge of solitude. At the hot pond rock I crouched down to watch the water slipping from the crevice, flowing and swelling, and the wind riffling the pond. Glancing up from the rock, I saw that I was now surrounded by a wavering sea of sky-high field grass.

From there I went on to visit the burr oak, so craggy and splendid of branch and bark, and discovered that it was host to a spreading colony of creamy white meadow anemones. The immense triple ash by the cartway had cast her dark flowers to the earth now. Leaves, big enough now for easy recognition, hung from the maples. I walked for a stretch beside our stone wall. Losing the idea of time, my tired feet trod slowly, patiently over the cracking clay of the old cart track, while a queer, midday sun forced down on me through the clouds.

The next afternoon we went to our lawyer's office for a meeting which dragged on late. The phrase "margin of safety" came up. Among the unedifying things we learned was that, quite simply, one cannot be safe against trespass and cannot be certain about the common "lake access" land, which we will share with as many as thirteen other lot owners. It was amazing how much effort and analysis of detail had to go into the simple buying of a lot. Because there still were things to be done, it appeared that the much-wished for closing would yet be extended for some time.

On a Friday at the end of May, late in the afternoon after Barry finished work, we went over to clip the grass around the baby trees and flag them. It was a golden afternoon, more early summer than high spring. At first it was hard to even find the little spruces in the thickening grass, but we worked away, pleased by the buds we found, a little troubled by the browning tips of some. We were surprised to see how many we had planted, and were able to imagine them in a decade, rising up to guard the front of the property. All the tiny green new-growth was precious. Except for the plaintive whistle of one train, there were only us, the trees, leafing out still more, and many birds. We worked our way around the orchard field, where we could see that the newly planted dogwoods were leafing out. What fun to imagine them as a thicket some day. Sadly, so far the red oaks did not look well. We passed the wildflower island and heard and saw a snipe proclaiming his territory from the top of a snag. This wonderful bird, with his ridiculously long beak, was sounding and looking much as the one used to who perched on a telephone pole outside our kitchen dooryard at the park house. On our walk I kept wanting to stop simply to look and listen, drinking in the extraordinary loveliness. Late that night in bed, I thought that in that most beautiful meadow I could see God walking.

Soon after, I had a falling-apart day, beginning with over-powering grief about the loss of Merak, the human-imprinted red-tailed hawk. As I wrote in my book *A Wing in the Door: Life With a Red-tailed* Hawk (Milkweed), Merak had been illegally captured by a would-be falconer. She was confiscated by a Ministry of Natural Resources officer and turned over to Kit Chubb at her Avian Care and Research Centre to "rewild." The spring of her second year, when she still had her brown tail feathers, the immature hawk was released at Foley Mountain in hopes that she would become completely wild. Sadly, Merak turned out to be too imprinted on humans ever to entirely lose her dependency. But this meant that for sixteen years we had the wonderful experience of living closely with a red-tail who flew free, but saw us as her immediate family.

The problem was that as soon as we knew we would be moving, we worried about what would happen to this beloved bird. Hard as it would be to leave her, we knew that the best solution would be if the new Area Supervisor wanted to watch out for her in her familiar setting at the park. Although the magnificent but psychologically damaged bird could hunt for herself, we always kept an eye open for her and welcomed her visits to our house, the centre of her world. In winter we got frozen lab mice from Kit Chubb at her Avian Care and Research Centre and stored them in our freezer, along with road kills, to supplement what she could catch, although we never knew for sure how essential this was to her survival. But if staying at Foley Mountain was not possible for her, then what?

Tempting as it might be to bring her to the valley at our new home and release her there, already we were sure that the other hawks we had seen considered this land as their territory. What chance would a seventeen-year-old, somewhat dependent red-tail have there, even if she could adjust to the change?

In early May this dilemma resolved itself. After her usual fruitless egg-laying, during which she produced only one infertile egg, possibly a sign that she was aging, Merak was savouring spring's pleasant, easy weather. One evening she flew in just before sunset, landing with her usual smug-sounding thunk on our back porch window box. Pleased to see her, I hurried out and stood by her, feeling a rising wind whip around us, blowing my hair and stirring her feathers. Although I usually tried to avoid being affectionate with her, in the vain hope that she would become more wild, that evening something prompted me to bend over and kiss her lightly but fervently on the small feathers on the top of her head. She, in turn, "gawed" at me, sounding pleased by my affection.

Then, without warning, in the middle of the night a tremendous thunderstorm cracked trees in the nearby woods. I shivered, listening. As always, all I could do was trust that this beloved, quirky bird would safely weather the savagely flashing lightning as she had many times before.

But Merak never came again and we will never know what her fate was. For days we scoured her old haunts, the great pine tree across the field, the sheltered forest at the campground, the lookout at Spy Rock, and the flagpole down at the Interpretive Centre, where I once met her riding out the gusts of another storm. Only with her absence did we fully and painfully recognize what an exceptional gift her presence had been for us.

When we heard a red-tail call in the field behind our farmhouse, Barry shouted her name over and over again. We watched that hawk circle near us, but it never dipped its head or appeared to recognize us. We watched and watched until it disappeared from our sight, trying to take in the sad lesson that our own beloved red-tail, from whom we had learned so much about hawks, was no longer there. Always we held in a tiny back corner of our minds the faint hope that Merak might reappear to us some day.

Shakily, I came down to meet Barry for tea and suggested we might go to the land for a brief walk — ostensibly to see if the wild cherry trees were blooming there. It was another of many changeable sky days, with stark, fast-moving white clouds, set against a grim, dark sky, with the grass and trees wet and the air saturated. All the trees were in glorious new full-leaf now, except for the oaks, whose red mouse ear leaves were almost too small to recognize as such yet, although they did have their catkins. As soon as I arrived I felt the solace I needed pouring into me. We walked slowly down Violet Hill and skirted around the water meadow, pausing to appreciate the creamy white flowers on the wayfaring tree we had planted the year before. We found the flattened grass of the lying down places of two deer, too. The landscape was amazingly changed. The pine trees on the ridge were no longer the centre of focus, and the birch trees were almost obscured by the abundant greenness. Now, it was the oaks and the big maples that rejoiced the eye, although actually there was beauty everywhere we looked. The rocky island in the field appeared bigger and more important now the leaves had filled out. Around past the rain-swollen pond we went, past the triple ash, down to see the foamy white-flowered choke cherries, and the burr oak with its field anemones. On the way back we climbed Box Hill, which we hadn't done since Easter, and sat glorying in the view. I left Barry sitting in peace and wandered a little further along the trail through the woods, wishing we had time to explore more. On the way down the hill, we imagined camping there in August and watching the stars wheel across the big sky. Hearing the veeries' music, I turned to look back up the hill with the big maples looming over it. In the meadow below, a song sparrow sang very close to me; the orioles were dashing everywhere, and we thought we saw a rare black, yellow, and white bobolink nesting. After one more look at the newly-shaggy fields and at the mallards and redwings nesting in the water meadow, we ascended to our house site. Meanwhile, the herons flew silently over our heads in their passages back and forth from pond to bay. There was a brief burst of sun to the west, followed by sprinkling rain pattering on the leaves.

After a series of cold, blustery days, the sun suddenly flooded through, leaving everything beautifully rain-washed. Tempted away from our work at the park, we went for a late afternoon drive to revisit the far side of what now would be *our* lake. As we passed boarded-up cottages, I thought yet again how fortunate we were to live in this area year-round instead of stealing brief visits as cottagers must do. In the fineness of early summer, wild apple blossoms were everywhere and now the lilacs were full and the honeysuckle, too. Imagine missing these. The heavy fragrances came blowing in the open windows of the car. We threaded among the many bays, seeing in a drowned swamp of driftwood a line of uncommon map turtles jammed together on a floating log, easily seen with their shiny shells. In places, waves from the overfull lake whipped, while in others, out of the wind, the water was calm. Everywhere there was the beauty of June fields, stretching to the sky, with blowing grass rich in many greens and that of trees now fully clad in their lush new leaves. Year-round residents, who were out cutting grass, waved a greeting. We belonged there.

As we drove, I was beginning to have a feeling for the topography of the area. Over at Buck Bay, for instance, I could see farms with lots of exposed rock, then sandy hills with many little farm sand pits, then into the woodlands and richer fields nearer our new home. All the cottage areas had different flavours to them, but each had a real sense of community, perhaps because people were there to be happy.

A few days later, when I took my friend Joy to see our land, we experienced a shining moment when we saw a fine, bushy red-gold fox with a handsome brush backlit by the late afternoon sun. All the creatures Barry and I had encountered at Singing Meadow behaved the same way. None of the twin small deer, the fox, nor the many birds were afraid. They were more mildly curious, as if studying us to see who was there now. This afternoon, the fox, in his turn, stood looking and then turned slowly and trotted purposefully down the Deer Run.

Suddenly, at the beginning of June, we received a call from our lawyer to say that we must close our deal immediately or the property would be put back on the market at an increased rate. As I hurried into Westport the next morning to get a bank draft and deliver it to the lawyer, I felt swept by astonished radiance. This was it. The beginning of a dream come true. It was a superb June day, warm in sun, cool in breeze and shade. The dooryard robins were bustling furtively over worms. There was the scent of lilacs on the breeze. The wren was calling its throaty summer song.

When I returned home, I decided to steady myself by planting potatoes. With red Molly basking loyally in sunny earth beside me, I plunged my hands into the rich deep soil we'd nurtured, and which had nurtured us, for so many years. While I was tenderly placing the long purple sprouts, I was thinking how very happy I had been to have this vegetable garden to care for. Ever since our very old neighbour, Stan Crawford, drove up the first year to show us the best place for our vegetable patch, on what used to be a pile of sheep manure, we had eaten well from our garden. My heart overflowed with memories. I recalled pitchforking out the heavy fieldgrass on calm evenings once our two little boys were asleep, proud of building our garden myself. In the distance, as the air cooled and the sky paled, I heard happy sounds from the campground where Barry was teaching evening programs to the school children staying there. Later, I remembered gardening accompanied by a series of beloved dogs, and also being assisted, after her perverse fashion, by Merak, the hawk. I recalled watering in the evening after hot days, feeling the friable soil soaking up the water which came from our well deep in the ground, gathering great baskets of sun-warmed tomatoes to freeze, planting Green Bells of Ireland with Jeremy while he sang a goofy version of *Moon, moon, bright and shiny moon, please shine down on me*, and sitting on the front porch with little boys in summer shorts while I cut beans to freeze. All those summers. How the field grasses went singing around me while the pink petals fell from the wild honeysuckles, and now and then a large yellow tiger swallowtail butterfly drifted by to dip into the wild purple lilacs.

That day, although I was daunted thinking of having to start again, I was deeply moved. I couldn't quite take in that Singing Meadow, another lovely place, was being given into our care. I felt cocooned in a silence of wonder. When I had slipped into town on my important errand, the people I had told were truly pleased for us. What did I feel? A little scared, but also touched by people's happiness for me.

That afternoon I returned to sign the papers to make the land ours at last, and then I sailed into the driveway, with a bottle of sparkling wine for Barry and me to share later, radiant with the relief of actually owning the land we loved. Barry quite agreed that we needed to celebrate, so after he finished work we drove over to the land, which now was truly ours, and went for a slow walk. Now we could afford to make plans.

A turkey vulture sailed low, dipping her wings over us as she caught the breeze. Molly tunnelled valiantly through the tall grass, following us. When we reached the triple ash, we loitered. We could easily clear out a few dead, low branches, and make this a fine, shady sitting spot, overlooking the meadow and the pond. We visited the burr oak, standing like a solitary guardian in the midst of the water meadow. On the way back, the male mallard, with his glossy green head, flew in close to us, alighted on the pond where he glided, and was joined minutes later by his mate. Even as we passed, the pair did not stop swimming, at peace, as we were.

Soon after that, though, I became seriously ill with pneumonia. Weak and miserable, for days all I could do was lie, studying the turning of the posts on the spool bed in our guest bedroom, where I had been relegated by my cough. Idly, I glanced at the book titles on the nearby shelves, books which, for once in my life, I didn't wish to read, or stared at the dancing boughs of the Norway spruce outside the bedroom window, or, most often, clung to June bird song.

Finally, though, there came a day when I couldn't stand being away from the land. Barry was using a few of his holidays to work clearing brush over at Singing Meadow and I persuaded him to let me come to keep him company. Reluctantly, because he was afraid it would be too much for me, he agreed. When we arrived I was amazed at how much had changed in the weeks while I was bedridden. The road frontage, where the clay soil recently had been scraped for the road allowance, was now thronged with daisies and wonderfully fragrant clovers, which were lush and warm in the heat of the summer sun.

Even though Barry carried my folding chair for me the short distance to Violet Hill, I could hardly find the breath to follow him. Unable to argue, I set up camp there while he strode off down into the valley. For a while I simply gazed in rapture at the wonderful lush water meadow. Eventually, though, I was lured to take steps, just a few steps, then just a bit further. In a pool of the wetland I was delighted to discover two wetland plants I had never seen before, and also heard many unfamiliar bird songs. Everywhere around me a sweet breeze was sailing through the grass. Unlike at the park, where the swarms of persistent deer flies were maddening, here there were only a few. Slowly, a bit at a time, I walked back to where Barry was working. Here, I sank down, surrounded by a sea of yellow and orange-flowered hawkweed. Around me danced more butterflies of all sizes than I had ever seen in my life. Although I found it hard to accept meekly having to sit without doing any work to help, simply being surrounded by such beauty brought me to life again.

That summer we were floating in a very tippy boat. Just as we had seen with both our parents' places, once we knew we were moving, things in a house that is about to be left seem to break down more frequently. Or is it that they irritate you more? The unsatisfactory sump pump arrangement in the basement of the park house broke one day, uncontrollably spewing sudsy water from our laundry around the basement. Uncharacteristically at odds, Barry and I stood roaring at each other in frustration as we watched the rough cement and dirt basement floor slosh with dirty, soapy water. The mould, the dust and the mess in the old farmhouse bothered me more than ever, both because they made the house unclean but also because I suspected them of causing allergies. Then one day while I was preparing breakfast, the front of one of the roughly-built kitchen plywood drawers fell off its loose nails one time too many, while two lower cupboard doors flapped open involuntarily, flinging out cans. And of course there was also the infuriating stove, with its unhelpful cast-iron burners, which on a humid day refused to boil eggs, and which never could bring to a boil enough water to cook pasta. Upstairs I crammed bedding into shelves that fit badly under a sloping roof. But all the same, I was troubled to be leaving the so lovingly arranged hominess and history we had made in the supervisor's house and I couldn't help wondering whether I would be able to recreate that feeling at our new place. Would we ever feel at home in a house, which, although certainly new and clean, would include pressed-wood baseboards and laminates instead of our farmhouse's hardwood and pine flooring? Every time I got attacked by nerves, though, I remembered to think of the land there, and then my lodestar was in place again.

Once I was well again, my hunger to be working on gardens and to be clearing the little woods behind our house to make vistas returned, stronger than ever. In my dreams I was transplanting some of our wild blue irises and some ferns and even planting some periwinkle in the woods. Unfortunately, the pneumonia had forced me to face reality. I now doubted that I could cut the large saplings, and I couldn't use a scythe or a gas brush hog, and I certainly couldn't dig heavy field turf. All the same, I yearned to do more to claim our new home with my hands as well as my heart.

As I studied the hard lessons of patience and possibility, I was on the threshold of acceptance that what was already growing at Singing Meadow was more than enough. I wanted to transplant burr reed to the heavy clay soil of the wetland. However, if this interesting plant didn't grow in our meadow, a number of interesting sedges already were there waiting to be identified and enjoyed, plants which, I was to learn, were key to the abundant butterflies we discovered there. No doubt the adaptations were subtle and I would be wise to learn from what was already succeeding before I considered introductions. For instance, high summer had obliterated the charming small stretch of stone wall that bordered the forest. This wall now was hidden under high grasses and abundant grape vines. But then I started considering: did I really want to remove the grape vines laden with the fruit that would feed birds and animals?

Following the wall, on a steamy midsummer day, we slipped into the dense woodland that was so evocative of my childhood home in the woods — the smell, the dampness, the rich feel of leaf mould beneath my feet, the evershifting dapplings of light, the soft stirrings of wind a long way overhead. But this land that we were only beginning to get to know was different too: very much a Lanark county woods of maples, with a high, airy overstorey and woodland grasses beneath.

Thinking ahead to afternoons spent quietly sitting there, I imagined how simple it would be to set up my old striped hammock as a moveable summer observation place the way naturalist Edwin Way Teale wrote of doing in *A Naturalist Buys an Old Farm*. Less doing and more being, I reminded myself.

Beside us rose a steep cliff with impressive mossy outcroppings. Ahead of us the sun lit the elephant-grey trunk of a beech tree of fair size. We had expected that the herons at the pond would be safely fledged. However, the most special moment of that lovely woodland interlude came when we found ourselves, thanks to our ridge vantage point, almost at eye level with two enormous, fluffy heron chicks, hunched submissively in their nest of sticks, guarded by a leggy heron mother. As we slipped through the shaggy growth to get a better view down the pond, we saw a few more nests still in use. Perhaps the late wet spring had delayed them. For a wonder, the mother didn't appear too distressed, so we stood motionless for many minutes watching this intimate scene in the still, early afternoon.

In August, new friends Charlie and Debby Stewart kindly invited us for dinner at their Bobs Lake island cottage to welcome us to the neighbourhood. While Debby prepared our meal, Charlie took us out on the lake to see his favourite places from the water, including the cliff at the narrow entrance to Crow Lake where young people dove, the osprey nests on tiny rocky islands, the best fishing spots, and even a bay that looked back to our development.

Wonderful hosts, Charlie and Debby kept us listening to anecdotes from their many years summering on the lake until long after the orange sun faded from the sky. Then, deftly threading his way through the dim islands of a lake we now knew a little better, Charlie ferried us back to the mainland by the light of a crescent moon.

Excited and happy about the prospects ahead, we decided to stop at our place before heading back to the park. Although by now the slim moon was extinguished by heavy clouds, along the cartway by the pond we watched late fireflies dancing and listened to the meadow singing its night song of katydids and crickets.

"Imagine, fifty trees!" Sitting at the hairdresser's later in the week, I was amused to overhear an Ottawa woman who was excited about buying a summer trailer lot that included fifty trees. Listening to her enthusiasm, I realized all over again how fortunate we were at Singing Meadow. Although our twenty acres was only about forty percent wooded, I couldn't begin to count the number of trees on our land, each one precious.

As August drew to a close, our ripe fields were stippled with golden black-eyed Susans. Saturday morning, squeezing the trip between groups of company, I dashed over to the land in the car with big blue camping water containers. It had been dry now for more than two weeks, and although we knew our soil was rich I worried about small young trees with sparse roots. For two hours I trudged through the rough and lumpy high grass of the fields with a heavy, sloshing bucket in hand, visiting each precious tree. Tipping the cool water around each one, I was surprised and pleased at how well the parched soil absorbed the water, and, for the most part, the young trees appeared to be doing well.

As always, working there gave a private, inward lifting to my heart. Eventually, I sat down in the shade to gulp my own water, and was rewarded with the sight of a large doe in her summer brown coat, shadowed by a spotted fawn. The doe was serene, but the fawn stamped at me and raised her white flag of a tail in warning, looking foolish with a Queen Anne's lace flower hanging from her mouth. But neither deer showed any sign of leaving, as would the more naturally wary ones back at the park.

When I left for home, I noticed that Terry Bryan, the real estate agent in charge, had pasted sold signs on the maps at the entrance to our development. There were more sold than I had expected, including the last two good lake lots, which was both exciting and worrying. The area was starting to close ranks or come together, depending on how you looked at it.

After our latest round of summer visitors left, we set out for a walk along the rocky ridge, or *mountain* at the park, a place we had not visited since the spring. To our sorrow we found that many of the oaks, both young and old, that grew where the granite was so close to the surface appeared to be dead. In earlier years, we had never seen damage like this. It looked as if the after-effects of the ice storm, followed by the debilitating drought the previous year, had been too much even for the tough oaks that grew in this inhospitable area. What was more, without the protection of these trees, it would be harder for new things to establish. Although I felt acutely disloyal, there was a part of me that was thankful that we would be living in a place where the soil was richer and the land was more sheltered.

We had a fine talk with Terry Martin, who was digging foundation and septic cavities for a couple of the lake lots near our land. As always, he had lots of gossip, some of which concerned his experiences of evidence of First Nations people in the area, and which particularly interested me. One time when he was working down by Wolfe Lake, he said, he had found an area with many rock piles that looked exactly like burial mounds he had seen on a television show. Also, a visiting archaeologist told him of a cave on the north shore of Bobs Lake that had paintings in it.

Reading Lloyd Jones' *Living by the Chase: The Native People of Crow and Bobs Lake*, I had learned that a group of First Nations people came to the lakes at the end of the last Ice Age. In the Woodland Period, about 5000 B.C. to A.D. 1000, there is evidence of clay pottery, but it is not known whether there was agriculture here. Jones writes that it seems likely that the First Nations people who would have passed through our land were hunters who moved to take advantage of available prey. In the time of recorded European history, Iroquois were followed by dominant Huron. By 1701 Ojibwa, known in this area as Mississauga, occupied Eastern Ontario. Then, in the mid-eighteen hundreds, a small group of Algonquin and Nipissing people left their main tribes to come to our region in search of better hunting grounds.

However, what I learned only left me wanting to know more. I couldn't help feeling that there was much more of a web of First Nations' life in this region than had been recorded. Certainly, throughout my time in Westport, I had conversations with many long-time inhabitants who revealed aboriginal ancestry, which they generally kept secret. How doubly tragic it was that not only were our earliest people frequently taken advantage of and relocated by Europeans, but, worse, that those who remained were made to feel such shame and fear that to this day they preferred to keep that proud ancestry hidden.

That autumn, on what I thought was the most beautiful day of the year, I decided I would take the day off from my writing and spend it at Singing Meadow. I scurried around collecting lunch, a silver thermos of water, sewing, my journal, and my favourite camp chair, hurrying before I could renege on this uncommon pleasure. At the turn-off to our land, I felt a flush of happiness. First I drove up to the lookout at the peak of Hemlock Hill, in the other section of the development to take in the astonishing beauty of the painted countryside.

A slight, cool breeze from the lake was sending leaves spinning down. There were fine mahogany-coloured ash trees everywhere, and the maples now were beginning to change. At the house site, I dropped my bundle of amusements and set out, intending to visit the pond and perhaps the little hidden meadow near the back of our property, which was bordered by an ironwood forest. I scrambled up the opposite bank and through the ironwoods, actually discovering the far northerly-western boundary stake, which we previously had not been able to find. At this point, I decided that, since a year had passed since our previous walking of our bounds, it might be a good thing to repeat this. And so I continued, greeting all my favourite things, going to the burr oak, the triple ash, the hill maples, watching clouds of minnows flickering in the pond, as well as the small, red, late meadowhawk dragonflies dipping in and out of the water there, mating. Then I walked down the cartway with the hot sun on my back.

Back at the house site, I spread my canvas chair, ate my sandwich with relish, and lay half asleep, marvelling at how tranquil and safe I felt there. Over at the park, I knew the autumn colours would mean a chaos of tour buses, school buses, many cars, and staff in and out of the barn behind the house. A pair of red-tails passed over the valley, soaring and touching each other with their wings. Deeply moved, for a long time, I stayed watching them, rejoicing in their wildness, remembering Merak, the familiar hawk who would never fly down the sky to me again.

V

Breaking the Soil

It was an important day, near the end of October. We were standing at the house site in a cold, steady rain, ready to stake out the dimensions. Paul, our builder, with his red jacket and a black Lee Valley fireman's hat, and David, his assistant, in a colourful yellow rain jacket, moved nimbly, measuring, stretching string to define corners, and whacking in pegs. Terry came across from the other house site where he was working to join Barry. What I noticed most was all the men's sympathy for us. After all, this first step of staking what would be our home was surely one of life's great moments.

Although I would not have let on to the men, my emotions as I watched this simple, traditional measuring and claiming were akin to those of the astonishment of hearing bells ringing for me at my wedding, or the wonder of seeing my babies for the first time. In a sense, we were marrying this land and the house that would enable us to live there.

Meanwhile, in the back of my mind I was thinking that this house-building would be an adventure that would require of me cooperation, participation, working as a member of a group, leadership, and direction: all skills that I would need to sharpen.

Soon after, tempted by a mild November morning, I slipped down to visit the park beach. Set against the backdrop of a lovely pewter sky, the late rising sun was the palest orange. For the first time since spring, water was running down the stream that flowed below the hillside waterfall. On the woodland trail beyond the Interpretive Centre, there was a soft haze in the air. High in the tall canopy over my head only a few oak leaves remained, waving from the tops of the bare-branched trees. Through the forest I heard the twitterings of many unseen late migrants, and at my feet two red squirrels involved in a kittenish chase dashed across fallen oak leaves. Down the steep hill to the lake, I went running and skipping over the tea-scented fallen leaves until I reached the lake.

Here the sun was bursting out like joy; it was a time of shining across the lake. The wind and sun were running towards me along the water. Close to shore, goldeneyes sped whistling over me, winter ducks. And further out in the lake a late, distant, low-flying flock of geese passed, followed by two more, hurrying after the rest with hollow calls. Near the far shore a solitary man was anchored in a small fishing boat.

My purpose, if I had one on this beautiful mild day, was to look again for beech drops, a strange parasitic plant like the ghostly Indian pipes of August. Ignoring the steady thrum and rush of traffic from the highway across the lake, I listened instead to the slightest lapping of water as I headed along the trail beyond the sand. Past the queer, muscled trunks of the blue beeches, ironwoods rather than true beeches, more shrubs than trees, I trotted. In the narrowing bay, the wind-driven water was smacking the shore with intermittent slappings. Six protesting mallards flittered out to join other rafts of migrants safe in the middle of the lake.

And there they were, an enchanting small garden of sprays of the pinkish flowers of beech drops. As I pulled out my hand lens to take a closer look, the wind rustled around me in the remaining ghostly bleaching beech leaves, while tendrils of wild grape vine clutched at me, holding me there.

Later that week, because the room layouts for our house were still somewhat fluid and unfixed, I began exploring what was possible. It was a given with any project that you must jettison some of your early work before its true shape appears. Certainly with our plans for a house, we kept finding this was true. Just as our former real estate agent Henry Connor insisted we would, we had changed our idea of the possible and in doing so ended up with something surprisingly different from what we thought we were looking for.

I meditated once more on my hopes and wishes. My central image was of simply sitting in utter stillness, looking out through the trees over the valley. With every fibre I hungered and thirsted for this. But it seemed equally necessary to have openness and seclusion in our house. How would we welcome visitors while preserving our so necessary solitude?

Resorting to graph paper again, I spent an afternoon testing how furniture would fit in the rooms we were planning for our new house. I was no longer sure about what to include where. For instance, did I want to squeeze my big old piano into the already crowded living room? Did I want my smaller floor loom in our bedroom, where it would be easily accessible, or should this room be kept simply as a bed and sitting place? (Fortunately for me, Barry always accepted a loom as a reasonable part of bedroom furniture, so the choice would be mine.)

When it came to a possible layout for our living room, I was stymied. The problem was that we were asking too much of a small room. We needed to locate the woodstove where it would direct heat to the rest of the house without making us uncomfortable when we sat in the living room. We wanted seating facing a small television, but also more seating for visitors. To make our decisions more difficult, one end of the room was taken up by windows. Although we had started out thinking of living with light and ever-changing views of the nearby Glade and the valley below, there was a cost for this in terms of limited wall space. Finally, Barry stepped in and solved the problem. We could have one couch looking at the woodstove and view and another looking at TV, he suggested, sketching them on the page with pencil so I could see what he had in mind.

Inevitably, though, uneasiness pushed up. We couldn't possibly know enough. And what were we forgetting? What would make us shake our heads later on? We were committed to a big process and one that would change the life of this land and its creature inhabitants, as well as ours, forever.

Over and over what I returned to was the recognition that what mattered to me was soulfulness. For now, although I wished I could resolve these dilemmas, I was content to keep reopening them gently, then setting them aside, trusting that good answers would come. If I adhered strongly enough to what was most important, surely the whole project would come together.

One night Terry Martin stopped by to get Barry to sign the application for our septic approval, which he hoped to get in spite of the relentlessly rainy fall and now-frozen ground. They stood in the doorway talking for a few minutes. "I hope you've taken pictures," I heard Terry say, "because once this digging is done, there won't be any point in filling the holes back in. You have to realize that it's never going to look the same again."

Another day, when I went for a pre-work walk along the park road, I heard the ice booming on the Little Rideau Lake to the south of me, and I made up my mind to drive to Bobs Lake in the afternoon, hoping to hear the forming ice sounding there too. There I walked the loop leading down the cottage road and around past the boat launch, listening to the wild beasts racing far along the lake under the ice. I was alive to the binding of the lake in its wintry chains. Each time that the travelling shrilled and boomed under the ice it sounded different.

Because I wanted Barry to hear this too, we drove over the next day after work, racing westward with the swiftly setting sun. Already the hollows were filling with darkness. Although we just missed seeing the orange ball slip behind the islands, we were filled with awe by the greatness of the light fading before the night. This time we walked out to Land's End, but heard only occasional ice sounds. At the tip of the point we were surprised to find a stretch of dark water still remaining open. Across the bay we saw a scattering of house lights in what was otherwise a fine wilderness or desolate coldness, depending on how one looked at it.

On our way back, we spotted a solitary man working on setting the large squared logs in place on a new house further down in the development. In what was quickly fading to darkness, we heard the grinding sounds of Terry Martin's yellow bulldozer, hurrying to finish before the coming cold and snow.

Always up and always down. In a snowstorm on a Sunday night we trudged happily to the park campground and back before bed, watching in the flashlight's beam as the snow came flocking down. Standing under the great pines, our joy for so many years, listening to them stir and swell in response to the snowstorm, I felt a choking regret to be leaving them. Although it helped us to know that we would be able to return easily to the park and its trails, we knew that the immediacy and intimacy of these impromptu walks would no longer be possible. It was unlikely that we would ever again stand under those pines on a winter night hearing the snow sift down through the boughs.

On a mild New Year's Day I heard the unexpected, touching sweetness of the nuthatch's spring song through our open bedroom window. Later, when I sat with tea, reading Clare Walker Leslie's excellent book on nature journalling, *Drawing Closer to Nature*, my eyes kept being caught by movement outside this window. First was that of five passing deer checking our bird feeder, but also there were the almost constant fluttering wings of visiting winter birds. This was so unlike Singing Meadow, where mostly we found that the spaces between life and the silences were large. Here at our park home, over long years, we had created a complex web that was intertwined with our presence and fuelled by our reaching out to other lives. In so doing, we were as nourished as the creatures were. I was thinking most of the two giant cottonwoods, which gave us joy with their beauty but also sheltered our house. They were looming presences that had stood by us when all thought they would die, surviving terrific assaults by ice storms and long-lasting droughts.

The night before I had been reading that studies showed that house plants did better when in the presence of their owners, rather than shut away, and better when they were actively loved and cared for. Surely this extended to the trees and rocks and animals and birds. Our caring notice brought them close to us and, in turn, renewed us. Symbiosis.

It was January 5, and our project was finally starting. Sunday, the phone rang just as we were getting ready to leave for our land, hoping to beat a promised snowfall, which would make walking more difficult. To our great pleasure, it was our builder to tell Barry that he had already put the house plan onto the computer and wanted to meet with us the next week to firm up what windows we wanted. How exciting that he was already working to make our house happen. Now, after the long stasis, things were moving. Now it was really time to think both about what we would like, and about what we could have.

VI

Moving Ahead

A few weeks later, we met with our builder to begin the planning process. When Paul couldn't answer our questions about window prices, he encouraged us to meet with him at a window wholesaler's where we could see examples and get a thorough explanation. Buying the windows ahead of time and storing them would save us money, he explained. Most generously, he waived the customary builder's cut of the wholesale window price to help us. Standing in the doorway before he left, he emphasized in the friendliest way that he believed that he could build the house with the money we had and that we would be pleased with it, and we, in turn, stressed that we wanted him to be happy with the project too.

This window buying went wonderfully. The salesman who met with us was helpful and encouraging. It turned out that for very little more we could get far more window than we had hoped for. The main ones would be taller and wider than we had expected, and we could have a casement window for the kitchen.

Home again at the park, Barry stretched up in our living room in the twilight, measuring out for us what windows for our new one would look like, and we were jubilant.

After we walked out along the park road to feed the birds, deer, and turkeys, I asked Barry if he would like to go with me to the land. I wanted to keep up with the weekly offerings of sunflower seed that we were scattering in select places there, I told him, but I also wanted to see where the sun would touch at the house site on a winter's morning. Willingly he fetched his compass and the sheet he had drawn up comparing the locations and times that the site was lit by sun, and we drove over.

A sparkling hoar frost from the previous night still lingered on the trees, particularly in Thrush Woods, which was backlit by the rising sun. I was pleased to see that feeding places had been scooped out and that the seed I had scattered there was mostly gone. From the gully trees I heard a few chickadees, not yet the flocking numbers I hoped for, but a promising sound all the same. As I had suspected, by ten-thirty on a winter morning pretty much the entire house site was in sunshine, and Barry pointed out how the light would flood my planned writing room. With the strengthening sun warm on our cheeks, we admired the site from every angle.

Then we ignored the fierce subzero cold (even the sunshine was cold) to finally go for our long-promised snowshoe hike up Box Hill, beyond the meadow. We approached the pond from the trail, remembering being there on a blazing summer afternoon when we were grateful for the cool, damp woodland shade, while we watched the herons loitering near their nests. The last time we went to the pond was at Thanksgiving with Morgan, when it was coloured by the surrounding autumn leaves.

This day, the bare-branched trees were reduced to black and grey, standing out over sparkling white snow. Because the shores of this pond were tightly ringed by steep rocky hills, it had been almost impossible to circle around it when the water was open. But now, after a month of hard freezing, we were able to snowshoe straight across the ice, pushing through the powdery, wind-blown snow, walking under the herons' giant stick nests. And because some were clustered out of sight at the far end of the pond we were pleased to discover that there were even more of these than we had thought.

As we headed up the steep hill after that, once again we were in new terrain where the going was quite tough. Because there were so many saplings plus rocks only partially hidden by snow, we abandoned our snowshoes, leaving them upright in the snow to wait until we came back down. Plodding through drifts of knee-deep snow was as good as meditation. Holding our breath, as we clutched trees for balance and eluded sharp, half-buried rocks, we couldn't stop paying attention for a moment. One slip, caused by the icy layer under the thin surface covering of snow, could hurt us. Then, when we were most of the way up, I suddenly saw, rather than heard, snowmobiles rushing past, right at the crest of a hill that we had imagined was in the back of beyond. So that was where the new snowmobile trail passed, that close. We hurried up the remaining steep edge of the pond and burst out on a well-used track.

Right behind the heron pond was land as special as any in the area, with hollows and forest and even more ponds. I was excited to think what this might look like next spring. We turned right, or south-east, keeping a careful ear open for approaching snowmobiles and set off easily along their packed trail in our boots. Just one more curve. Just one more rolling hill. Just to the handsome, spreading oaks ahead. Along the way we found marks in the snow of what looked to have been a bounding fisher, as well as the drag marks of a travelling porcupine. On and on we walked, completely forgetting the sharp cold until the red-gold light began slipping away, ascending the hills, the treetops.

Returning to our snowshoes, we slid back down the hill and across the frozen pond to the glorious sweep of Box Hill, where we saw four pixie-ish deer clinging to a Vermontish rounded little hill, a primitive painting waiting to be made, while we watched the setting sun. From there we made our circle, coming out into the sunshine of our little meadow, inevitably being drawn to our little spring-fed pond, which was almost frozen but not quite. The larches we had planted last spring were completely buried by snow, but I made out the tassel of one baby white pine on the slope of a back hill. Our discoveries were as encouraging as the strengthening February sun on our cheeks.

Back at home, after I wrote down my notes about the morning, I pulled out the topographical map for another look at the ponds on our land. What fun it was to be able to discern each ridge, each trickle of water we had discovered on our frosty hike.

Within a few weeks, we were back at Paul's for another meeting. After three hours of solid work, we finally signed a contract with him, and I believed that in general we all felt good about the results, although I suspected that all three of us felt battered by the intense, important negotiations. On our side, as we had expected, some things that mattered to us would have to be given up. At this point it appeared likely that there would be no cold cellar and certainly no pine window frames. The doors and baseboards and trim would be the moulded ones that Paul dismissively called "paper": the floors would be laminates, all of which would be plain and skimpy, adequate but unworthy. Indeed, at this stage it was looking as if our longed-for home would be crafted mainly of false, cheap-looking materials that we believed to be aesthetically wrong, and worse still, unsatisfactory from environmental and health standpoints. My first thought was that it seemed as if there was little left of the carefully planned house that would express our personalities and provide a home for spirit. Yet wait a minute. Stop and think. In many ways the home where I grew up, with cheap blue linoleum floors in the kitchen and hall and poor, neatly painted plywood kitchen cupboards, had been far from satisfactory, yet what an enchanting home it had been for me.

Among the many things we had achieved for our home were a woodstove, pleasant workable rooms with fine windows, a helpful, pleasing kitchen, room for tools and books, and, most essential, the land. For Paul, too, the commitment was tense. Although he did not say so, at this stage, he also must have had reservations. Likely he was thinking how risky the complex process might well be for him.

On a morning walk along the park road, we met Terry Martin sanding it, and spent the better part of an hour gossiping cordially, but also got his reassurance on a number of worrying questions. Meanwhile a pileated woodpecker flew past us and drummed on a tree just off the road. Eventually we saw first him, and then what must be a mate, judging by her pleased response to more drumming. The impressive woodpecker was sending chips flying briskly.

I should have been at home writing, as had been my habit for so many years. But then, after the house was done, I told myself, and we have moved away from the park, we likely wouldn't see Terry often, and we would miss these times. Perhaps it was best simply to stop and take pleasure in our visit.

Seeing the flash of the pileated's sunlit red crest, I was reminded of our Afghan Kilim rug, another of the purchases we had made for our new house. The woodpecker's crimson was exactly the main colour. We bought this carpet a few years ago when we saw it at a bazaar, blowing softly in a November wind: one of many hung on racks outside, swept by snow flurries. "Choose me. Choose me." So we did. And it had been waiting for us rolled away ever since. How would I describe the carpet's deep, glowing red, I had asked myself. This morning I knew.

In a piece of foresight on his part that would save us many later expenses, Paul had asked us to go to Rona Hardware to order our kitchen and flooring. Buying before the spring building rush would mean that the store would guarantee the prices and would hold our materials for us to be delivered at the right time, with no delivery costs. But before we went, although in theory I was committed to simplicity, I had to deal with some moments when wanting nice things for my home gave me a brief, evil rush, as from eating too much sugar. When, for example, I was browsing in a high-end woodstove store where I was surrounded by top-of-the-line, charming treatments and accessories, such as a wall of fieldstone, or a pretty red stove kettle, I felt a wave of lust. Moreover, as a craftsperson myself, I would have liked to add much that was handmade to this house, and I would have liked to support craftspeople. Occasionally I imagined a bathroom in pale earth and grasses colours, which would bring the outdoors in. The basin I unrealistically coveted for this bathroom was a handmade ceramic one I had seen in Maine, which was encircled by little brown shore birds. At such times, a few low-relief handmade tiles found their way into this imaginary bathroom as well.

Of course, the reality of what we could choose was much plainer, but all the same we were pleased with what we found that morning. We ordered louvered doors for the bedroom closets, and acceptable laminate flooring. After our meeting with Paul, it was looking as if we would be able to lay basement flooring after all, so we chose *cherry* for that and *oak* for the upstairs. (How I disliked using wood names for products that had never seen a tree.)

Wednesday we met with the township building inspector, who was kind and reasonable. He told us that we could have our building permit in two weeks; however, to satisfy him we would have to get an engineer to design the frost floor that would be required in front of the patio door, and we would need a basement floor drain. Otherwise he just asked Barry to fill in a few extra measurements on the plans Paul drew up for us. We would need at least four site inspections, he told us, and were required to get license numbers from all *the trades*, as Paul called those who would be working on the project.

At the beginning of March, Bob Stewart, who would be a neighbour, phoned to ask permission to harvest a jar of minnows for bait from our little pond. This early in the season he couldn't reach those in his part of the lake, he explained. What was interesting was that he told Barry that our pond had always been a pond, but was dug deeper five or six years ago, and in fact was now fifteen feet deep in the middle. Apparently the minnows there were different from any others in the area and indeed had not been identified yet. Bob thought there also was a large yellow perch in our pond too. There were fish in the heron pond behind us as well, but not like these. He agreed with Barry that one of the features of this place was that there was water everywhere. He also mentioned walking way back through the land behind us to where there was a big waterfall, which a farmer had funneled in with lumber. Bob was friendly and helpful, offering that we could dock a boat at his place, and he would show us how to navigate the complex system of islands on the lake.

Next, Barry phoned another neighbour, Jerry Thompson the well driller. Jerry cheered us by saying that he didn't expect our well would need to go deep. If the bedrock was white granite, as much of the area was, he would do a pounded well, and if there was sand it would need a filter on the pump. Otherwise, he thought it should be fine and said to call him when it was possible to walk on the land, and he would come to take a look. Then, when Terry had been able to put in our driveway and culvert, he would come and dig our well for us. Now, with the first intimations of spring, many things were starting to come together.

Giving up on our vision of a wood-clad house, as we now knew we must, had been hard to swallow. The last thing we wanted was vinyl anywhere: not doors, baseboards, or siding, both for ethical and aesthetic reasons. How many more compromises would we make, we were beginning to ask ourselves. In the end, would we feel that our house reflected us?

So now, having given up on the idea of wood siding, we were reduced to deciding which insipid vinyl colour would be least offensive. Grudgingly, we borrowed a sample book from the hardware store, took it to the house site and held up the rubbery sheets for each other to consider. In our woodland clearing, cream was too light. We thought that it stood out too much. The blue-grey sample appeared gloomy, and the beige was simply sickening. A second set of very dark samples did not make our choice any easier. We just didn't like anything about vinyl and found it hard to commit to this. Also, we were trying not to think of environmental issues such as off-gassing from the vinyl and how toxic the manufacture of the siding is for workers, and how unsatisfactory the eventual disposal of this product would be. As house owners, vinyl siding would be a sensible long-lasting, trouble-free choice. But for all its convenience, it was one in which we took no pleasure.

Meanwhile, friends were still trying to inspire us into better environmental choices. Although at this stage we were reasonably set in our plans, we wanted to make sure we had explored every possibility. One Friday evening in March, we were invited to investigate a straw-bale building owned by new friends. Jerry and Eleanor's adobe-style studio was certainly attractive, but they were candid about the amount of heavy work involved, and confirmed what we had suspected: that it had been as expensive to build as any other kind of house. It was their own inviting old farmhouse that tugged at our hearts. They had refurbished this just enough to be comfortable. Everywhere new, simple but good windows highlighted pleasant farm views. Good unobtrusive lighting helped too. There was a spacious kitchen with a big, old cookstove, a snug, low-ceilinged living room, and bedrooms painted in interesting colours.

At this point, the chaos caused by the constant planning work on the new house was making me feel so befuddled that I was forever making my daily chores harder for myself. Already I had cut up a current credit card by mistake and thrown out the recent Sears catalogue, just when I needed it to plan curtains. All the time Barry was asking me not to let him forget things, but in this jungle of far too many details, I could not promise to remember. Both of us were on edge, and it didn't help that a number of our friends were envious and others thought we were spoiled. Shouldn't we be excited and happy to be having a brand new house?

As site supervisors for the project, we phoned and got our contractors' names, addresses and license numbers, and then we went on to phone about an additional kind of workmen's compensation that Paul thought we might need. Fortunately, because we were not a company, this turned out to be unnecessary. However, privately I was questioning how much security one needed and thinking with regret of what has been lost with this complexity of regulations. I was remembering how people used to invite their friends to help them shingle their roof. How would neighbourly barn-raisings, such as the one Barry and I helped with long ago in Cobden, take place with so much emphasis on regulations?

The weather on the next weekend was miserable, so we had no wish to go outside. When Barry suggested that we should tackle the attic of our park house, I knew it was time. In the summer, working in this uninsulated space would have been intolerably hot, and anyhow by then we expected to be too busy at the new house site.

When we opened the half-sized attic door for the first time in years, so strong was the wind coming through the poorly insulated attic walls that a drift of snow blew in on me. Immediately I was overwhelmed by the litter left by mice and the piles of far too many boxes.

Funnily enough, though, sorting proved to be surprisingly easy. This was because most of what we had thought was worth storing turned out to be useless. Why had we imagined we would need to save cheap beer glasses, hideous surplus china, endless flannelette blankets, mostly of single bed size, and Barry's outdated school texts? Nevertheless, the work of sorting and discarding was charged with nostalgia. Indeed, when I pulled out Morgan's little rust-coloured fringed cowboy jacket, last worn when he was three, I came to tears and was unable to throw it away.

We did turn up a few treasures. For thirty years I had missed Grandma Guard's little globe vase, etched with strawberries. In the same box, I also discovered my grandmother's silver, jewel-studded mechanical pencil from her school days in the late eighteen hundreds. Barry was pleased to dig out missing letters and a special wooden box given to him by his father. All the same, I was surprised by the things I didn't remember, and I was still more surprised that the memories felt so definitely over now, and not regretted, either. It was much more interesting to be living in the present.

While Barry carried boxes out to the truck and I plugged away back at the attic, I amused myself by reflecting on the many different approaches to building I was experiencing. It was my wished-for hall window that was troubling us now. It had already caused a fight, and even I was no longer sure whether my plan was wise. Instead of having the writing room closet stick out across the end of the hall, I wanted to keep that three feet between our bedroom and the writing room open and place a long, narrow casement window there to add light and make a floating view over the gardens.

I saw this casement window so clearly that it hurt. What I wanted was to add a little magic to our otherwise plain house. When I sounded Barry out though, he was vehemently opposed, protesting that it was ridiculous to give up much-needed closet space for something admittedly frivolous. But as I shoved tattered boxes of old textbooks out the attic door, I had to admit that I didn't feel ready to give up on the window and all it would mean to me.

At this stage in the process, understandably, Paul wanted to consider that our design was final and Barry wholeheartedly concurred with our builder. After a recent battle with me about our plan, he emphasized that all he wanted was closure. His wish was to make decisions as quickly as possible and then to adhere to these. (For emphasis here, he enunciated "No more changes.") My approach, which involved playing with ideas, piling them on, shifting them about, always rethinking and refining, was merely frustrating for the two men.

Although neither Barry nor Paul, both of whom were up against tight realities, would have been interested in what I read in Christopher Alexander's architectural bible, *A Pattern Language*, my need to be fluid about designing our house seemed more reasonable. Don't rush the process, Alexander stressed. He suggested that we keep adjusting the original design to accommodate new ideas. "Don't be afraid of making changes," he insisted.

In the following days, I continued to have difficulty working out with Barry how to achieve at least a few features of beauty in our house. As he prepared for the busiest season at the park, this was a particularly bad time to approach him, but I longed to revisit the idea of having a hall window at the southern end of the house. Being tied to memories of my childhood home, where I had watched cardinals courting from a similar long window, this appealed to my deepest instincts. Also, I thought it might be special to be drawn down the hall by the light, and to see our lovely clearing framed in all seasons and times of day and night from what would be a high vantage point. I was remembering how when I was very little, I pushed open my upstairs bedroom casement window to look down on my realm, Rapunzel-like, from on high. I thought of an outswinging window as an invitation to the out-of-doors. To me, this casement window was true to the very idea of home and what it should mean.

But, stressed as he was, Barry continued to be cold and stern. He had asked me to make no changes, had told me how much that mattered to him and I had not respected his wishes. As far as he was concerned, the house plan was finished; it was not negotiable. What was more, the very idea of losing any space inflamed him. We left it that we would quickly decide once the framing had started.

Unfortunately, at this tense time, between house-building chores and the arrival of his busiest time at the park I suspected that there was absolutely nothing I could propose right then that Barry wouldn't flatly veto. As for me, on the other hand, I was feeling that this might be my last chance to put a stamp of me and what mattered to me on our new house.

But when, at the beginning of April, Terry Martin told Barry that, if the weather wasn't excessively rainy he thought that he might be able to prepare the driveway for us in two more weeks, we completely forgot about such details.

VII

Underway at Last

It was May 3, and at long last the physical work of preparing our house site was under way. There were tiny showers, but the cold day meant that there were few blackflies. As I began the notes I planned to keep over this exciting time, Terry Martin was preparing our driveway. The scraped topsoil, which he would save to spread on a lawn later, looked rich and thick and fluffy. He did find a slick clay base near the road but fortunately not much in the way of solid rock. Bending over to examine Paul's neatly planted boards, marked 4'6 *here* and 2' *here*, which he had carefully set out to delineate the exact dimensions of the foundation, he muttered "Not many put in batter boards like these now, but it's good that he did."

Later in the morning Jerry Thompson, the well driller, pulled up in a big shiny new maroon truck to check in. Right then, Jerry was drilling at the log house beyond us. He and Terry were easy and friendly with each other, and I eavesdropped on their conversation. The two talked another language I didn't know, describing local geography to me in a way that was foreign, considering everything in terms of how feasible roads were. There was a brief digression about the dastardliness of Hydro reps, usury, and five hundred dollars for a thirty-five dollar job. From here, the talk moved on to bad ankles. Terry mentioned that in the past he once sprained his ankle at his farm, put duct tape on it and carried on. That night he could hardly get his boot off — and indeed the pain still hurt. Wouldn't be surprised if he had broken a bone, but wouldn't go to a doctor, wouldn't consider it. After Jerry drove off, I prowled around, sniffing the smell of the rich, fragrant, wet earth and marking with yellow survey tape the trees we had planted in hopes of keeping them safe. From there, I wandered happily down across the valley to the ironwood forest beyond in search of wildflowers. Always in the background I heard the beeping and careening of the digger with its

blade attacking our driveway, and before long I was drawn back to
see how the work was progressing. So far Terry had removed two
big boulders with little real problem. The driveway was scraped
now, as was most of the soil from the house site.

Soon, Terry's brother and employee, Eddie, arrived and asked
me what I thought of it all. When I remarked mildly on the noise, the
men took pleasure in assuring me that the annoyance now was
nothing compared to what lay ahead: the truly dreadful, relentless
pounding of the well driller. When I ask what drillers did with the
slurry they dredge up, they grinned. "There'll be two guys staying
there for a week with the rig. You'd think while they were hanging
about they could take a wheelbarrow and shovel, but many don't.
Most often, either people step in it or it ends up right in their
driveway."

Before he left, Terry told me that he was surprised to discover
that he could still feel the remains of frost in the ground. For now,
the field grass gave him leverage for his heavy machines, but he
feared that after it was scraped off the excavation site tomorrow real
digging would be too precarious. "It's still too soft, but likely it'll be
all right," he said in his Irish lilt. Actually, there were cautions all
afternoon, if I had been able to read them, "ground surprisingly
wet," "ground still too soft," "quaking like a bog."

Late in the afternoon, Terry and Eddie drove off to fetch a big
digger so they'd be ready for their seven-thirty start the next day.
The birds were quiet, no doubt shocked by the day's violent activity.
In fact, the only sound was a distant train.

When I woke the next morning, it was cloudy and only zero
degrees Celsius. By seven, though, the sky was clearing and there
was a sharp wind. Driving in to the development, I found I was part
of an exciting parade of trucks, all coming to work on various sites.
When I arrived on the road outside our lot at seven-thirty, two
trucks were parked on the grass, a transept was set up, and Terry
and his nephew, Allan, already were busy working, while Eddie
was busy greasing the digger. Disappointingly, the northwest corner
of what would be our basement only went down four feet before
bedrock. In theory, there should be six inches more, but everyone

assured me that this discrepancy was nothing, only a mere six inches to be added on to the height of the house. "If you don't do your corners you can get yourself in a mess. I think we've got it," Terry told me, "but it's going to be close." Overhead, two osprey were calling and calling. At the house site there was a sense of tension, energy and effort, but also of something important being born. One consideration was the flow for the septic, which Terry knew had to be high enough at the west end. There was much jumping into the hole and holding up the yellow metal tape measure for someone, usually Terry, to sight from with the transept. In the beginning, Terry planned to use the big bucket on his digger, but he was finding too much rock, which might damage its teeth. Having to use a smaller bucket meant the excavation would take longer. The layer of big boulders, something Terry was afraid of, would mean we would have less topsoil for later. Some of the boulders could be used to make a foundation for the driveway, he told me, while some would get piled at the west end of the house, to be covered and graded later.

Careful and thoughtful, Terry and his two "lads" worked easily as a team. Meanwhile, David Pollard showed up on his way to another site where he was working with Paul just now. Helpfully, he suggested grading the slope from the basement walkout so we wouldn't need stairs down to our patio door. Before he left, we stopped to listen to the exquisite calls of a loon.

By ten o'clock Allan had about half of our basement dug. Every now and then Eddie used a shovel to smooth out the floor. (Already the earth surface had become a floor.) They checked the accuracy of their work frequently, using a long piece of white plastic drainage tile with the level resting on its top. This was delicate work, where Allan just fingered the soil with the bucket of the digger. Precisely at the stakes that delineated the edges, he made incredibly neat slices. At one point, I couldn't suppress a gasp as he wallowed his machine through the soil, maneuvering with astonishing ease. With his big front tires actually off the ground, he balanced as delicately as a dragonfly by flinging out the machine's extra bracing feet.

For a while, trying to avoid being conspicuous in my watching, I sat on a little wooded rise, making notes as best I could with my fingers stiff with the cold. To my surprise, the violation of the earth didn't trouble me as I had expected it would. Meanwhile, across the way it was satisfying to see the sun filling the whole house site. A white-breasted nuthatch flew in and scolded softly beside me.

As the morning moved on, Terry continued to work scrupulously on the driveway and watching him brought me a new understanding of the meaning of patience. I was seeing that with Eddie and Allan too. The clumsy-looking machines really were extensions of these skilled workers, who in their intensity and attention, seemed to become what they were doing.

Looking beyond the house site, I turned my eyes to the handful of blooming daffodils I had planted in the woods along the Deer Run and wondered whether they looked unnatural there. Some of my time I took pictures and wrote notes, while some of it I sat or prowled in a contented daze, thankful that today, at least, it was too cold for blackflies. Much of the time, I happily hauled brush and piled it. While I did this, everywhere I glimpsed trillium shoots springing up through the thick bleached carpet of last autumn's maple leaves. I also was discovering much bellwort, and also the blue-green umbels of bloodroot leaves, which I was at least as fond of as their milk-white flowers. Tiny maple leaves were out and, deep in the surrounding woods I was delighted to discover a wild honeysuckle and, even better, one solitary baby beech tree, which I hoped would prosper in the shade of our new house.

At eleven, Terry walked me out along the driveway, jumping a bit to show me how the saturated soil quaked. It was spongy, he warned: wetter than he had expected. We were lucky, though, he said. They hadn't found any rock that required blasting. We walked back up the future driveway to look at the neat cavity they had made. "You've got yourself a beautiful spot," he said again. "It's a natural. Private and yet close to the road." He talked about grading and slopes, envisioning what was ahead with his experienced eyes. "We'll clean it up for you. I won't leave it the way some folks do." Already I was wondering whether this was builders' talk, buttering you up, so you'd take the fall better. Nonetheless, I appreciated the kind words. Terry had been with us right at the beginning, encouraging us to choose this site and we both felt safe with him.

On the following day, because it was raining I decided that, rather than hovering at the site watching the roadwork and the digging of the septic hole, I would pack up my spinning wheel and fleece and join a small gathering of friends for a day of handspinning. This time, the monthly event would take place in the big, beautiful European-style house that my Swiss-Canadian friend Dorina and her husband had built when they emigrated here. An experienced house-builder would have cautioned me that being absent from a house site was always unwise, but I didn't know that then.

I greatly appreciated Dorina, with her warm heart and love of nature. Anyone who would rejoice in camping out by her large pond solo from May to October was surely a kindred spirit. Most of all that day I loved being in the presence of her house with its great floating windows looking out on the delicate tiny crimson and green spring leaves, creamy birches, and rain-washed pond.

After lunch, a few of us joined an informal tour of Dorina's house. It was affirming seeing her precious things, a flax wheel, a handwoven rug made by a friend in her nineties who still happily crawled under her loom to tie it up. As we explored and talked, different considerations surfaced. One was the need to include ties to our childhood memories of home—for example, the contentious hall window for me. I blurted out that I was having more trouble getting Barry to agree to this window than anything else. Ears pricked up, and all the women exclaimed in an unexpected unison, "If it's important to you, you insist on getting it. Otherwise you'll wish you had all of your life. Sometimes you just have to." I came home cheered and smoothed, with Dorina's gift of an unusual orchid-coloured violet for what would be my new garden. Thanks to my friends' advice, I did ask for, and get, the hall window, though to

this day, people remain divided about whether gaining the view and
light was worth losing the storage space.

    Just as earlier peoples sometimes carried ashes with them to
start new fires, I wanted to bring a few precious little trees from the
park to plant. So the next day I came to Singing Meadow with a
moistened burlap sack stuffed with some rooted cuttings from the
honeysuckle bushes that grew wild there, along with a few
butternut seedlings that we had purchased from the Conservation
Authority and, most important, some white pine seedlings. After all,
the superb old pines were one of the reasons we fell in love with
Foley Mountain. There also were a few of our favourite shagbark
hickory nuts, which we hoped might take root at our new home.

    But when I arrived, I was startled by the alarming, unexpected
sound of a chainsaw, followed by the toppling of trees. While I had
been absent, without warning the septic hole had been moved to a
little wooded hollow directly east of the house. But digging there
had meant that the crew had had to cut out all the trees, not just the
few hawthorns and basswood scrub I had expected. Eventually, I
knew we would get used to this, but for now it was hard to accept.
A robin perched on the stump of a cut maple, which was weeping
sap, looking as distressed as I felt. Although nothing was said, the
men clearly were aware that we would not be pleased by this
change of location, and there was a lot of explaining of how much
better this would work. Since Eddie had his chainsaw with him,
sucking in my breath, I asked him to wreak further havoc, cutting
out the slim aspens on the far curve of the house site to open that
area for sitting. His nonchalant speed in doing this was both
wonderful and dismaying. Although I knew how much we would
enjoy this small clearing, watching trees crumple, I had to accept
that I myself was attacking our beloved land.

    Badly shaken, by nightfall when I was back at home in the park,
I surprised myself by beginning to cry involuntarily. The truth was
that I didn't like all this heavy machinery work on our land.

Although the work being done was actually straightforward and minimal, the whole project felt like a bucking bronco that could easily get dangerously away from us. It was Barry I turned to for reassurance. Only he knew how fragile this building experience was for us. With amusement I was recognizing that we were entering a new phase in how we related to each other during the house-building process. I was amused to find that now we had become a defensive alliance. At this stage we had nowhere to turn for reassurance but to ourselves. All we had to protect ourselves was our mutual interpretation of the gesticulating, inarticulate language of builders and excavators and their joint strategies. One thing was sure. If we were going to be involved in house building, I was going to need to toughen up.

But in spite of the present anxieties, all I needed to do was recall the constant blessings at Singing Meadow. When I was there, blue jays slipped around me, flashing knowingly among trees with leafy young buds, a heron's shadow skimmed by me as he flew low overhead, a mourning cloak butterfly flitted across my path, an azure butterfly danced in the steamy heat over the masses of violets down in the sward. A song sparrow sang its exquisite song from the valley below.

Driving over early on the loveliest of May mornings for the first day of actual building, I stopped a minute by the line of fine large maples which marked the entrance to the development, looking at the rolling pastoral hills lined by tumble-down rail fences and the sky blue bay across the road. Look behind me, look ahead: There was beauty everywhere.

Because I was early, I visited the boat launch lane. I hadn't been there since last fall, before the snow blocked it. Here I took a few minutes to rejoice in the sparkling lake and the fragrances of cottage country — damp earth, sunlit cedars, and lake water.

I had been rather dreading this first building morning because I still was learning how to negotiate with Paul. In case big trucks needed the new driveway, I decided to park below in the valley and walk through the swaying fieldgrass that was growing by the foot. Here in the light morning breeze, the smell was from rich earth, moist from yesterday's rain and now meeting hot sun. When I reached the site by this back way, the newly risen wind was reaching the sparkling lime green aspen leaves. All about me I heard the joyous-sounding "okalees" of redwing blackbirds. I dumped my knapsack, heavy with cameras, notebook, and lunch at my chosen vantage rock, which I hoped was a discreet distance from where the men would be working. As it turned out, Paul was excellent at helping me to understand his plans, drawing the loose information into a tight, skillful ball for me. And while he was telling me his plans for the next few days' work, a loon flew right over our heads, calling exquisitely.

The schedule at the moment? Friday pour footers, Monday frame walls. But before this could be done, the building inspector would have to come and approve the six neat footing boxes the men were creating. He would like to have floor and walls done by end of next week, Paul told me, and then, the following week, have the basement floor ready to pour.

Later in the morning I asked Paul roughly when he thought he would be done building our house. He took a minute to outline what he was planning. He would finish closing in our house to the door locking stage, and then would turn it over to the electrician, plumber and heat contractors while he went to work on other projects. Then he would return later in the summer to do the interior work, he told me.

Meanwhile, I was noticing how easy and consultative with each other Paul and David were. As with anything at such an early stage, though, they were slowed down by the great amount of planning and calculating involved.

At first, I cleared more brush and took snapshots of the footings. In contrast to the machine noise of the past week, Paul and David were making tranquil, workmanlike sounds. When I got too red-faced with heat, I sat on my rock, munching an apple and making my notes, groping for what would be most evocative about the building experience, what would remain in my memories later. Around me, as I considered this, the orioles were distractingly loud.

I also traced a chipping bird to a high poplar, a male rose-breasted grosbeak.

Eventually, the redwings calling in the meadow drew me away to wander along the Deer Run, to the light and openness of the valley below, and then, ever so slowly, yet still not seeing everything I wanted to, I moved past fields dappled with purple violets.

When I returned, the men were packing up, done. We talked a bit more about schedules and ordering, and I felt reassured, smoothed. Paul offered that he had salvaged a good toilet and sink free for us if we were still wanting to rough in a basement bathroom. Touched and pleased, I said an enthusiastic *Yes*.

I arrived at eight-thirty the next day to find the impressive cement truck already on site and pouring cement through the great long chute neatly into David's wheelbarrow for him to trundle to the various forms. Paul forked the cement vigourously and smoothed it as meticulously as an artist. In the day's dense, humid air, the rich grey cement was so oozy that it was hard to believe it would harden. Here, where we were in a climate zone that was slightly more northern than Westport's, there were still many black flies, unlike at our park home where they were finished for the year. A lovely little cool lake breeze stirred the air and a hoarse, earnest-sounding raven hurried by on her way to the lake.

David walked over to join me, saying how talking to Terry reminded him how vulnerable self-employed men were. If an injury happened, there would be no pension, nothing to fall back on. All of us were worried by how tired and driven Terry was. Paul joined us with his natty stainless coffee thermos and perched on a rock near my own favourite one. At the other house site where he was working, he told me with mild reproach, there were bentwood chairs all over, and even a hydro spool for a table. Yes. I thought to myself. I should bring chairs for the men over here. We went over what would happen Monday: delivery of lumber, frost floor construction, and building walls though perhaps not erecting them. Exciting.

In spite of the pressing blackflies, I happily finished my notes and then went to put my new tree guards on the bigger of the transplanted trees. Wonderfully, even sticks of sapling spruces and pines that had appeared dead when we stuck them in the soil were now putting forth new greenery. I wandered up to the place where the well was to be drilled. Just behind it, the woods we would see from our living room was white with trilliums. From there, I slipped down into the valley and sauntered over to our little pond. A catbird was voluble from a nearby hazel thicket. Overhead, a pair of ospreys mewed to each other. Eventually, I forced myself to leave the house building and go back home, but I was looking forward to Monday.

When I pulled up at eight-thirty that day, though, Paul and David only gave me curt nods, as they were in the midst of a private indignation meeting. This was not going to be such a good day. It appeared that on his other project Paul and the owners had reached a complete disagreement on interpreting the plans. "She says it's there. But that is never going to work out. There's no way it's there. She's just wrong, that's all." These were people Paul respected, but at this moment, frustrated, he couldn't or wouldn't back down. Meanwhile, I felt small, meek and anxious, wishing to be much more the good child than I knew there was any need to be. How would I manage when we had disagreements here, as we inevitably would? What was more, on that touchy morning it came home to me that it must be very hard for Paul and the crew having me present with my stated purpose of writing a book. Although Paul had easily given me permission to observe, I suspected that knowing they were watched closely and that I could be reporting on everything they were doing surely made the work more difficult for the men. Although I tried to reassure them that I would never knowingly use my privileged vantage point against them, they often mentioned jokingly, "You're not putting that in the book, are you?" Perhaps my presence did slow them down, and they couldn't talk freely among themselves.

When the promised Rona truck arrived at nine with lumber, the driver and remote control operator looked like a university student with a summer job. All the same, I was amazed by the remarkable delicacy and precision he used, methodically preparing to unload the bundles of lumber and Styrofoam that would insulate the frost floor. For all the men, there was a meditative quality about their serious work. The truck driver dragged out bracing feet on each side at the back of the truck, set these on pads, and released the crane fork to do its work.

Everywhere in this situation, I was aware of possible danger. For example, Paul walked neatly under the swinging crane, and minutes later the crane whirled around precariously. With one quick, deft flip, the fork cradled the bundles in a jigging tilt. As David stepped over to help, I couldn't help thinking what would happen to his feet if one of the bundles of lumber slipped a fraction in its gentle lowering. Yet all went well, and the builders ended by setting the bundles gently and precisely on raised two-by-fours so that the truck's fork could be slipped out. In passing, David remarked to me, "You really wouldn't want to be under the crane when there was a rookie driver. It could leak a dump of hydraulic fluid." A kingfisher flew by very high, very fast, in a dipping flight, scolding his dismay, but not veering from his path. "Probably see you in a week or so, to bring the trusses and floor stuff," Paul called cheerily to the truck driver, who was sweeping the truck bed. Meanwhile, I returned to dragging brush from the woods. In the comparative silence after the beeping lumber truck has left, once more I heard "okalees" from the nesting redwings. It was surprising to me how much bird song continued in spite of disruptions. On one of his regular flights from the nearby lake, an osprey sailed by on a high current.

As I watched, the men were laying the sills, a setting up of the house's framework, which meant much thoughtful measuring. Watching their pattern being set up, I was charmed. These sills were actually reminiscent of my childhood games of "house" where I used a rake to shape rooms, which were delineated by leaf piles. They were working on the dining room right then.

When the work stopped at lunchtime I wandered over and peered into the basement hole. Two large framed units lay against the dirt walls. Over sandwiches, we talked briefly about plans. Paul was going to phone Terry about delivering more gravel. Although I knew it would be unreasonable to say so to the men, I was starting to get skittish about hearing "more" of anything because this inevitably lead to more money. I knew I needed to be flexible, and to resist the feeling that I was staunching a bleed that was bursting out of containment at many points. At this stage, though, the house build, with its unpredictable expenses, apparently had taken on a life of its own. It was becoming a machine that felt barely in my control.

The next day I drove over to the site early to meet Jerry Thompson, the well driller, who was a slim older man with steel grey curls and a shrewd, direct glance. Although it was only right for him to warn me that there is no guarantee in well-drilling, I was chilled to hear that a couple of the mandatory test sites on this estate actually found no water. Although I didn't say so to Jerry, privately I didn't feel comfortable having a well drilled without witching. It felt arrogant to plunk down your equipment where you wanted water without asking the land where it was to be found.

Only that morning, old Don, who sometimes worked with the Foley Mountain crew, popped into our kitchen early. Having heard our well drilling was about to start, he wanted to tell us about a farmer near him who drilled six wells and got nothing. "What did he do?" asked Barry with a grim tone in his voice.

"Well, of course he called in an old Russian woman with an egg," Don told him.

"An egg?"

Yes. She carried it around flat in her hand until it stood up on its own."

"'Drill here,'" she told him.

"And sure enough," Don said, as Barry rushed around the kitchen getting ready for the day's classes, "when they dug there they got water right away."

Then he went on to mention somewhat smugly that he too could witch for water. On a roll, he added, "Matter of fact, I know a technician who has a process guaranteed to double your flow or no money. Absolutely guaranteed." But when he added in that the additional cost of this process would be three thousand dollars I spluttered that I truly hoped we didn't get to that.

Jerry told me that the well at the newly built log house further down our road found a good flow of water at a mere one hundred feet. He added that he thought that people worried too much about germs. Often, according to him, letting a well rest a few months was all that's needed to sanitize it, "not ultra violet lights all the time."

A few days later, Jerry's assistant told me that he thought the pounder must have reached fifty feet. As we stood chatting, I was thinking about this probing so deep below the surface. Just what did a depth of fifty feet into the ground actually mean? If only it were possible to see where the drill was travelling.

Irritated by anxiety about how deeply our well would need to be drilled, it was a day when everything was bothering me—the well pounding, the slick mud around the site after all the rain, the seemingly chaotic building apparatus, even the men's good cheer.

When I heard a wood thrush calling near the house site, I decided to change pace and explore how our visible land above ground itself was changing. In the meadow, everything was rain-washed and wonderful. So rapid was the spring growth that the world here was being made new each day. Everywhere, there was shining and dancing from the clattering of newly emerged spring dragonflies to the clouds of darting tiny minnows in our small pond. Continuing on, I went to stand by the purling water at the grotto. Illuminated briefly by the high noon sun, this secret place was at its loveliest. The hill that hid this cleft was now dense with wild plants. I had never seen so many slim-spired mitreworts, as well as jack-in-the pulpits, and Solomon seals, both false and true, and three kinds of violets. While I listened to the music of the water hurrying to the lake, I was looking out on the small paradise of an enclosed wild garden with baneberry, trilliums now turning pink, lush deep green moss, and the scrolls of emerging ferns all caught in the brief illumination of the sun, exquisite.

Further along, I smelled before I could see a ragged, tall blossoming wild apple tree, its roots no doubt reaching into the grotto. As he flashed about, a vivid orange, the oriole was calling everywhere, and also I heard an oven bird. Far back towards the heron pond, the pileated woodpecker was sounding like a Japanese drummer. Everywhere, leaves were bursting out—maple stars, tender basswood hearts, burr oaks' mittens barely leafed, and ashes, too, just beginning to unfurl their mysterious black fist buds.

Moving further back to the hawkweed meadow, when I bent to retie my shoelace, I was delighted to spot a small patch of orchid-coloured gaywings, *polygala paucifolia*, a special little plant from my childhood that I had never seen since. If I had been earlier or later in the season I would have missed this happy discovery.

By the end of the week, there came a day of cold sun between two days of downpours. Slipping and sliding around the foundation on the clay, I was pretty sure that sooner or later I was going to do a pratfall on this slick earth. Interestingly, David told me he suspected there was a small spring beside the house. Standing and chatting with him before his workday began, I felt a real sense of a pleasant home being made for us. As he pointed out, the basement stayed good and dry in spite of the great rain last night. That afternoon Barry joined me at the house site just as the latest promised rainfall was starting. The clay was impossibly sticky, adhering to our shoes in clods like a slapstick joke. But as we looked around together we got two wonderful surprises. From the framing on three sides, we could see the beginnings of a house that looked big and tall. And then Jerry's assistant announced casually, "I hit water about an hour ago."

"And a good flow?"

"Oh yes, indeed. Plenty."

This was one of the big moments. At last the well pounding stopped, and we watched the astonishing free fall plunge as the water suctioner sank, then lifted again, racing a hundred feet. I stood staring at the magical water, drawn from deep underfoot, rushing, dancing out. This first, white-grey water sluicing out was to be tubed towards the valley. Jerry's assistant driller was closing up now. "It's the long weekend. Got to go and drink beer," he said cheerily. "You got a high production well. Could do a hundred head of cattle. Looks like good, clear water, too."

Behind us Paul was neatly writing his calculations with a marker on a scrap of wood. As he did so, I heard his voice lifted in indignation, as he complained to David about a troubling conversation with one of his other clients:

"So Marky called last night. 'Are you going to come tomorrow?' he asked me." (This was quoted by Paul in a squeaky falsetto.)

"No, Marky, the windows aren't there, so we won't be there. 'But there's lots of framing you could do,'" (Again, Paul reported this using his client's pleading voice.)

"No, Mark, no, no, no. We're not coming even next week. We're not coming until the windows are actually in the showroom. So far these guys of yours haven't been exactly trustworthy, have they?"

Meanwhile, Paul and David were measuring and measuring and checking against each other. Making this final basement wall and taking into consideration the south-facing patio door, with the necessary frost floor beneath it, looked to me to be the trickiest part of the house so far.

I liked the deft, careful way Paul put things together, checking each joint after he united it to make sure it was as good as could be. When I was a small girl, craning my neck to watch my carpenter grandfather and uncle framing houses, I didn't remember them doing this checking. Perhaps building was so ingrained in them that they didn't need to. But all the same it was reassuring to hear him doing it.

On the weekend, a sunny-thundery afternoon, Barry and I took advantage of a break in his teaching to come over and climb Thrush Hill. We had been reading L.M. Montgomery's *Pat of Silver Bush* aloud at night, and I said to Barry that we were like Montgomery's Jingle and Pat, playing in their special secret place, *Happiness*. Growing up, I longed for a best friend, someone who completely understood my love of nature. With Barry, I had that and so much more.

If ever a place could be called *Happiness*, it would be half way up the ridge, where the wonderful big hardwoods grew. After two years of good rains, even the rocky tableland at the top of the hill seemed lush with flowering hawthorns, starry twin flowers, frothy little Canada mayflowers and heaps of the tiny, orchid-coloured gaywings I had discovered on my earlier walk.

Extremely happy indeed, we scrambled back down the steep ridge to the immense white cedars nestled at the base of the ridge. Here we peered through the upended, clawing roots of former trees to a spring welling up. Farther along we looked out, through old white birches so large I couldn't encircle them with outstretched arms, to the little pond-meadow beyond the cedars, which was fed by the springs and which threaded its way through the low-lying field to become our water meadow.

The following morning was the first radiantly clear cool day in many. Down in the valley I was overjoyed to hear the snipe calling modestly but persistently. Close by, at the entrance of the Deer Run, a wood thrush was singing melodically. I was standing watching a Rona truck deliver more lumber when the third member of the crew arrived, having just finished his carpentry courses at a community college. Slim, dark Julian, the third member of the crew, was neatly dressed in black. He appeared alert and ready, but didn't yet have the instincts to help jockey the delivery loads around, and waited to be told what to do. Soon David turned up and began drilling holes in the concrete footings. The main job for today, he told me, would be putting up the central load-bearing beam, another defining stage.

I was finding that spending long days at the site suited me perfectly. A few years ago, after my mother died, for the first time in my life I was dismayed to find that I didn't want to go out of doors at all. In my grief, I lacked even that consolation. It felt to me as if nature was roaring outside, giving more stimulation than I could bear. More recently I had gone out, but only tentatively. Now I was thankful to be back to wanting to live outside. Once again, as I always had before, I wanted to become one with it. At last, after the dark time, I could hardly bear to come indoors and made every excuse I could to stay out.

Over at the site, the well-drilling noise had been replaced by the racket of a generator and a different drill grinding into the cement. For a while I sat in dappled sun beside a False Solomon's Seal and watched a brown funnel spider guarding her web. Beyond her, I caught sight of a partly moss-covered rock, streaked with pink crystal. This morning, I couldn't help noticing with interest a strong smell that I suspected might have come from an earlier visit from a passing bear.

Driven off at last by the noise, I took my new, sharp garden shears and stalked to the front of the property to trim the grass around the tiny spruces we had planted there. As I snipped, I was listening to cricket song and the carolling call of the oriole overhead. All the meadow flowers of high summer were coming along. The day before I found blue fragments of an opened robin's egg. Today, when I moved on to cutting down at the verge of the water meadow, I met the fat male robin, one of the nesting pair who knew me from our various projects working near the house site. It was bliss visiting the trees and caring for them. Each one was precious. Across the meadow I could see the black, white and yellow nesting bobolink plus an unidentifiable bird with a square seed-eating beak perched on a cattail. A crow flew by, checking to see what I was doing, then a blue jay. In the distance the newly returned yellow warbler was calling "witchetty witchetty." Over and over, I needed to keep saying that I felt deep down, richly happy in the meadow. In the glassy eye of the pond, water was burbling up in such a powerful spilling-over that it chuckled musically. Indeed, while there was such a flow only the boldest, largest minnows could swim strongly enough to approach the rushing source.

Before lunch I called an informal meeting with Paul and "the boys," as Paul's wife, Violette, affectionately called them, where Paul explained to me the work they planned to do next. This continued to be a tense time for them because everything had to be laid out right. Always there were so many calculations to be included, more than I could even imagine. But then, hearing a discussion of putting the big beam up after lunch, I felt a flash of excitement. Installing this massive supporting beam, which would stretch the length of our house, would mean difficult work over the men's heads. After everything was stabilized, Paul said, there would need to be bracing and strengthening to be taken into account. Listening, I had the feeling that Paul was talking the house into being.

After our talk, I went back to sit on my rock and eat my potato salad. Birds were flitting all around me, two tantalizing, unknown warblers, and the robin pair, who now were comfortable with my presence. Pausing, resting my eyes from the bright May light in the clearing, I stared up through the starry green maple leaves overhead, thinking that I loved these trees more each time I saw them. With pleasure, I watched the female robin neatly catch a moth from inside the big brush pile I had made, before she flew off to her nest.

Although I wanted to remain in the vicinity of our builders, I didn't want to intrude on their hard work. So, on a day of hazy sun, with heat and humidity rising off the field, I took myself off to clear some space around the pines we had planted high on Box Hill. When I finished this clipping I went further, walking along the cart track through the meadow with several woodcocks quavering over my head. Then, in a wet rut I met the snipe rummaging with his long beak. Further along the track I discovered a swift little stream flowing from yet another of the valley's many springs.

Perhaps the best part was the walk back. I had noticed with regret that I was losing that "falling in love" edge to my experiencing of our land. Today, though, approaching from a way I hadn't visited since the beginning of this adventure, I began remembering coming here for the first time. With a smile on my face, I recalled how we came to see Lot Ten on an August afternoon but were disappointed to find we couldn't make it work for us. Luckily, we continued beyond it into the broad, winding valley, discovering the loveliness of the hidden, sheltered meadow, lush even in a drought year, with the lone burr oak standing guard. How fine it would be to be able to live here, I remembered we said that day, but we doubted we could afford this most beautiful land. Once again that shining late afternoon moment grew vivid for me. And now, wonderfully, a large part of the meadow was ours, and I was walking happily, confidently over "our" land.

Sunday, when I was at home at the park, I brought my camera out to photograph the bark of our two cherished dooryard cottonwood trees. I wanted to capture them in both black and white and colour. What I was doing was saying the beginning of a passionate goodbye to them. I was kneeling and craning, playing with swelling sun and dancing shadow, getting inside the crevices, waltzing my eyes over the complex intertwinings of their bark again. Some of the sweeping branches would need drawing to do justice to them. I knew that. Still, working with them to capture their very essence, clicking swiftly, recklessly, I was drawn utterly within the trees.

Before long, I saw a beautiful three-and-a-half foot grey rat snake wind out from under Barry's truck. Sitting on the grass close by, I watched it glide up the cottonwoods, astonishingly pausing on the trunk with no apparent means of attachment, where it stretched its sinewy length on a limb over my head. These days I was exhausted with sorrow at the thought of leaving our long-time home. But even still there were many fine moments such as this encounter with the climbing snake. What was more, our shared grief also was bringing Barry and me closer.

How would we ever leave Foley Mountain and all the familiar creatures there? On this heavy, sad day I lay out under the beloved cottonwoods, our dooryard trees, staying with the magnificent snake all afternoon. The flowering shrubs that encircled my gardens there had never been lovelier. Scattered through the fields, wild pink and white honeysuckle were everywhere, more than I could remember seeing in other years, harbingers of plentiful berries for the birds, especially the catbirds. The air that blew around me was heavily perfumed by the immense purple flowering thickets of settlers' lilacs and also by the apple blossoms from the wild orchards and the lily of the valley I long ago brought from my childhood home.

All the birds, all the flowers that surrounded me were there largely because of us. The crows raiding the apple trees, the red-breasted nuthatches flitting, the blue jays flashing, uptilted in our sunflowers, the dancing sea of yellow daisies given to Barry by our friend Mary Jane, the surprising lavender autumn crocus, which I had watched spring from small brown bulbs, all of these had gathered me within them as I have taken them into my deepest self.

It would be no less than the truth if I said I knew the park land "by heart." In my forties I had been seriously and frighteningly ill with chronic fatigue syndrome. Most days I was too weak to do more than lie in bed. During that dark time, my thinking was so scrambled that writing became hopeless, and indeed I suffered from such exhaustion that I often couldn't even lift a fork to feed myself. Certainly, walking the dear, familiar trails of my world at the park was no longer possible. Many techniques and people helped me to get well again, but one of the most powerful ways I found of healing was visualization. During those long days, I had no way of knowing if I ever would truly walk the trails again. But if I could not take pleasure in walking freely as I had before, I still could retrace my steps slowly, lovingly, in my mind. During those long, frightening days, I recalled all the many, many beloved places there. And from this practice I gained strength. Only then did I know how deeply I carried the land of Foley Mountain within me. That afternoon, sitting near the rat snake, I knew that what I would be doing when we left would be no less than turning my back on a large part of the map of my heart.

By this point I had discovered that it was important for me to be present while the house was being built, helping it along in some obscure way. What was more, when I couldn't be there the house lost its reality for me. So the next day, torn as I was between work at the park and the building, I returned to the house site once again. Now Paul and David were talking about stair treads. "Eight inch risers and nine-and-a-quarter inch treads," I heard. "That will leave three feet at the bottom of stairs," Paul explained to David, "… more or less, depending, for floor joists and stuff." Using the imperial measurements he preferred, Paul had started a board and was using a stair guide (carpenter's square) to test (try) the stairs. Captivated, I hurried over. For each tread and riser, you would add between 15 and 19 inches, they told me, but also you had to take into consideration the steepness of tread and the size of tread and slope. Apparently there was a book of tables to help out. Because the stairwell leading to the basement was tight for room, our stairs would have to be fairly steep. As I watched, the men were slanting the board on which Paul had marked the stair angles, checking for level, always checking for level, and allowing for a four inch thickness of concrete that will raise everything at the bottom. Calmly, they jimmied the board up and down. Finally it was decided that we were going to have a turn-around landing at the bottom, with one step down from that.

While the men went on to other work, I was loving sitting on the footing by the opening where the patio door would be, looking up through a throng of white, new, sunlit joists. What happened next would depend on when Terry delivered a further half load of gravel. If it didn't appear soon, Paul and David would turn their attention to the upstairs, where I was excited to hear that in another week or two they would be ready to put in the windows.

Above me, I heard David and Paul working together easily like a married couple, anticipating the other's thoughts. Julian was away, picking up his first vehicle, a truck, and the other two seemed calmer, more natural, working on their own.

Later in the week, when I drove over to the site, the morning was cold, with splatters of rain. But I was happy to hear veeries, with their most musical of songs. Over my head, the woodcocks were whirring in sprinkling rain, while I could hear the snipe piping vigourously from the boggy meadow behind the house. Nevertheless I was feeling rather grim. I was learning that acting as "Site Manager" meant being at the centre of many problems. My understanding had been that Terry had some lag time to deliver the frost floor gravel. But when I met up with him that morning, Paul was looking tired but also determined because he said he had reached the point where the frost floor needed to be installed or there wouldn't be enough stability. Panicking, I drove way down the road to where there was phone reception and caught Barry just as he was heading out to a meeting. I urged him to try to reach Terry, explaining the seriousness of our problem. Then I returned to the site. Very shortly after, thanks to Barry's persuasion, Terry wheeled in with a dump truck. Problem solved. All the same, I was beginning to suspect that each bringing in of "the trades" would be hard to co-ordinate.

With peace restored for the time being, I nested in my vantage point behind the foundation and watched high, swift-flying clouds and listened to the reedy piping of our snipe as well as the sounds of the newly dumped gravel being shovelled level. From there I looked north, envisioning clearing a few scrub trees so we would have a view of the so beautiful valley. Then I twisted a little in my seat, appreciating how close the unseen lake was. My companions, the robins, were in and out of the great brush pile I had made, their beaks full of worms. From within what would be the house basement, I heard more consulting and measuring:

"That wall wants to be..."

"And then we'll figure out..."

Feeling unsettled by the earlier friction, I steadied myself by wandering back to the pond to spend a calming half hour watching the glittering minnows basking in the shallows. When I returned, Paul and Julian were up on the main floor, caulking assiduously, sealing, laying out plywood, sledge hammering.

Driving in on the private part of our road the next morning, just before the maple line, I was delighted to spot an impressively large, sulphur yellow-throated Blandings turtle at the side of road, digging its sandy nest. Of all the local turtles, the endangered Blandings ones have been my favourites since the first one we encountered trudging up the park laneway in its annual trek to lay eggs beyond our house.

At the site, I had an early morning consultation with Paul and David about window placement for the main floor. At the same time that I was discussing progress, from the valley I was moved to hear a pair of red-tails who were sailing on early morning thermals calling insistently. Listening, I felt a flash of sorrow for Merak, the solitary, human-imprinted red-tailed hawk who was too dependent on people to attract a mate. In the bowl of the valley, where the sun had barely struck yet, I heard, but could not follow, guttural calls of a raven, possibly hounded by crows.

Our house was becoming more house-like all the time. On this day, Paul planned to have the northern and eastern valley walls framed, he told me. Then, after our brief discussion, I wandered over to the Deer Run, where I looked down over the valley, ethereal in the misty sun. When I returned, I took pictures before the upper framing was set up. Because the day was pleasantly shady and breezy, I decided that I would shift my camp to the north side of the house. In my new perch, where I could look out over the sunny front meadow towards the beautiful tall maples bordering our property, I felt airy and pleased.

Paul was whistling cheerily and interjecting snatches of Spanish while he was marking the dimensions for a sill on a two-by-six. I overheard, "For every window height, seventy-seven and three-eighths, you need a bunch of cripples. And then we'll have it all ready to rock-and-roll." What with the whistling and now the sound of hand sawing, familiar from my childhood, I felt at home. Paul was moving lightly, as if he loved this part. All three of the men were content, sure of their places. It was a bit of a dance.

On this fair and rising June morning, looking from my new vantage seat, the house looked like a tall, imposing, spacious shelter for two people. I watched Paul comfortably, competently striding about, marking swiftly, surely. "Like we did at so-and-so's and such-and-such's houses," he noted in an aside to David about his measuring. There was history there.

It was nearly noon. I had clipped and dragged brush all morning in the rising heat. Now I sat writing an overdue letter to a friend, but also dreaming and delighting. Was it really I who was watching my house being built while I was surrounded by the splendid trees and meadow and hearing the golden, summery song of the oriole? "This is for me and Barry. It is not for parents, nor for our children, not for friends," I thought in wonderment. At last, incredibly and delightfully, it was my turn. This would be a place for me and my husband. It felt as if I had been climbing a long, steep hill and had come out in a beautiful safe clearing, where I could rest at last.

In the afternoon, the crew erected a steep gangplank leading to the end of the hall using various methods to jockey up two-by-fours and the more difficult, unwieldy plywood sheets. For each section, they built the frame then nailgunned sheets of plywood over it. So far, of course, there were no holes for windows. The men marked out top and bottom plates and made vertical chalk lines. Finally, on a quick "one, two, three" count, the three of them hefted the large, heavy frame they had been making. After that, with great care, they sledgehammer-tapped it into position, true on their chalk-line snap.

With the midday sun glaring on the whitish wood, it was blazing hot up on their floor. Paul burst into snatches of song to keep himself going, mostly stuff from *Cats*, dragged out to maximum nasal effect. I caught a feeling of all of the men pulling harder, almost instinctively egging each other on through the heavy, tough, careful work.

Meanwhile, in a blissful interlude I retreated to my leafy bower with my Peruvian basket and spindle. Sitting under a large maple near the capped well, as I twirled my spindle and twisted the painted cotton fleece into yarn, I fancied I could feel the tug of the heavy channel of water our well had tapped rushing far beneath my feet. The more I lived with this land, the more I was thinking of it as a place of many waters. There was the nearby big expanse of Bobs Lake, which once had been four lakes, but which after the installation of a dam flowed into one larger one. But also we had been discovering that this was a land of abundant springs and underground rivers, as well as tiny brooks, and ponds, and indeed the everchanging water meadow behind our house site. As well as the granite firmness beneath me, there was also the blessing of abundant, everchanging waters threading unseen under the surface.

At three-thirty, the long and ponderous truss truck, with a conveyor belt of rollers appeared. The actual dispatch of the two kinds of trusses off the truck was shocking. The premade frames simply got shaken off in stages and eventually collapsed with a crash in a heap located precisely in front of Terry's pile of dirt and rocks. The driver was a genial, tired (everybody was tired), old Scotsman, with neat white whiskers. Earlier in the day, he told us, he was north of Smiths Falls where he delivered to a site where a whole multi-generational family all were happily working on their future home.

Even overnight, things were happening at our house. Next morning I nipped into the basement to fetch plumber Brian Bond's fixture catalogue, hidden neatly under our future door as promised. The night before, long after we had all left for the day, Brian had passed by our site on his way home from a job on an island. On a day when even the birds were subdued in the face of the approaching heat, it was amazingly cool in the basement.

When I went around the back, I discovered another delivery: piles of sand, which must have been dropped off by Terry. Later that morning he arrived with a further load and then Allan arrived with the digger, followed by Eddie with a truckload of plastic piping. Noisily working at a furious pace, Allan was spreading the sand, maybe three or four truckloads. Once again I was troubled by the assault our home was making on this perfect spot. Allan's motions felt violent, and on the edge of dangerous, as did Eddie's ramming of his white truck towards our woods. Watching the mess this ground work was creating, I had to accept that landscaping would be impossible until the crew finally finished.

Untroubled by the row, dragonflies were skimming around the generator. As for me, I was trying to keep a clear head for my notes in spite of the screeching clatter of the swinging digger bucket and the generator's relentless thrumming. Looking up, I watched Paul up on the raised platform of our main floor, where he was doing a rapping Spanish dance on carpenter ants, while in the basement I watched David cutting out a hole for the patio door where before a panel blocked most of this space. At the slightest tap the panel fell away and, magically, we had a space that I could see would become a door.

Meanwhile, Eddie was sawing and fitting septic pipe: a lot of it. Pausing for a minute, he unwrapped and ate a slice of watermelon. He threw his shirt off, exposing a back nearly as red from sun as the melon. Although going shirtless was Eddie's own choice for coping with the heat, watching the men work hard and long in the fiercely hot sun, performing routine heavy work disturbed me. I knew many of the actions they took were damaging their bodies irrevocably. Just as I minded our project's damage to the land, seeing the attrition to the workers also was hard for me to accept. I was learning that in building a house there was an economy of costs that had nothing to do with financial sums.

The digger claw neatly flicked a septic pipe out of the way. Then its knuckle patted the ground smooth. Allan's chair swivelled and he whirled in it, examining all angles. Eddie was raking what was now a neat five-foot deep septic cavity absolutely smooth. A dusky-winged butterfly flitted up the sheathed side of the front wall. Meanwhile a stub-tailed chipmunk approached right up to me. I wondered whether he was in shock about the greatly revised little valley beside us, which was now a septic bed.

When I returned home that evening, Barry met me with the dismaying news that his student assistant, who had a painfully swollen throat, had just learned that she had mono. He had had to teach fifty children on his own all day, and there was no telling how much longer he would have to do this. Some classes would have to be cancelled or come on their own without an interpreter. That this was happening in his last teaching year, and when he had so much else on his mind made it intensely disappointing and difficult for him. At this crisis, neither Barry nor I had time to help the other. Even our three cats and Molly the dachshund were sad and reproachful because we had no attention to spare for them and were so often away from the park house.

The next day, when I heard the men prepare to hoist the other bedroom corner, being very careful because the breeze could swing the framing dangerously, I scurried around with a camera to take a picture. I remembered being warned about how confusing perceptions are during the process. This morning Terry and I had thought the house looked big. Now it was small again. As I photographed, there was work going on all over the place. At one point, I was amazed to realize I was standing in the midst of six men, all working for us on different jobs.

Made giddy by all that was happening, I went for a brief ramble along the lovely, lonely road to get some peace. The sweet scent of clover was heavy on the mild, moist air. On the house side of the road was the paradise of June wildflowers, and just a little farther along the other was a vista of deep blue lake stretching far into the distance. The profusion of June wildflowers now was astonishing. There were daisies whitening the roadside, masses of wild clover and hawkweed—much yellow, some a vivid orange. As for snapping turtles, for the last week or so I had never seen so many, likely because we were so close to the lake. One night that week, six had taken advantage of the sandy shoulders of our road to lay their eggs. In the soft shoulders of the dirt road I discovered eight fresh turtle nests.

As I rounded the curve, I reflected on all I would have to learn if this project was to be satisfactory for all of us. Sometimes, for instance, I suspected that the men understandably were exasperated by my lack of clarity when I had to give directions. The act of saying "I want" was new to me and I knew I would have to become more effective at being quickly decisive and making my wishes clear.

Even when I returned to the house, I decided to stay at a distance from all the activity, sinking down under the spreading ash tree at Violet Hill, gazing across the meadow, watching the wind running through the flowing grasses. My glance shifted to the nearby pink flowering high grasses of the wetland. Here all was shimmering, evanescent, exquisite. Only after the men left for the day did I go over to see what they had done. Standing beside the plywood-sheathed box, letting the rising breeze cool the sweat on my black cotton shirt, I realized that all the framing had been finished. At last we had a proper house. The next day, if the weather was fair, it would become more proper as the trusses went up. Then the next week our windows would be installed. We were getting closer to having our house. I could see it.

When I arrived at the site at eight-thirty the next morning, the place was seething with activity. Already all the plywood to cover the roof had been delivered, plus more two-by-fours and one impressive sixteen-foot-long beam. The men had built a sturdier gangplank, which they would use to schlep all the materials up to the main floor. For the first time I met John, the whistling electrician, who was very efficiently at work. Bantering with him, David fingered the various kinds of pliers swinging from a heavily weighted tool belt, which was perhaps the neatest, most professional-looking one at the site.

I could see that this was going to be a very different kind of day from the calm work pace of the three house builders. Today the patter and witticisms were flying mercilessly. It seemed that both John and David sang in bands. There were snatches of song and wisecracks about such favourite topics as the unhelpfulness of metric measurement and the misdemeanours of Ontario Hydro. While the men were setting up, Terry dropped by to make sure things were going well at the site. I sometimes suspected that, although he never interfered, he was watching out for us, keeping a careful eye on the younger workmen.

"Lay out sixteen-foot centres," called Paul. "Find out which way it wants to be, Julian. Towards me, David. No, just a bit." Although it was one of the days when everything was happening and happening fast, all the same, there came a moment when all of us, country people, paused to watch the hovering, piping dance of a single osprey from the very top of sky. As David had loaded lumber he had mentioned to me a surprise he had yesterday—a grass snake that turned turquoise at death—and I told him that I, too, had seen that gorgeous turquoise before.

Trying to ignore the fuming generator, I watched a large, clear-winged dragonfly subdue a still-struggling fly. Around me, I could feel the lovely day rising. Oh my. I glanced back over my shoulder and noticed the first erected room partition—one dividing the middle spare room from our bedroom—and I was thrilled all over again.

After noon, when the lunch boxes were placed back out of the way in the shade, the men turned to setting up the scaffolding so they would have the frame in place on which to rest the twenty-four trusses, which would need to be jockeyed up to form our roof. To do this, they erected two ladders so David and Julian would be able to walk the trusses up to the peak, where Paul would grab them. As the men worked, there was a discussion of useful knots such as the Round Turn and Two Half Hitches, which I remembered from my Girl Guide days. Julian had to take a knot course in college, he told them. The others kidded him about this, but only lightly. Then David changed pace, calling over his shoulder to me the news that before he left for home last night he had spotted a skunk digging up a nest of turtle eggs here.

"Cut twenty-two inch blocks for facers. Then start putting trusses up, put up nailing strip for drywall. With chop saw cut two-by-sixes or two-by-fours." Ignoring our chatter, Paul muttered his plans to himself.

Yesterday I noticed that the light had changed to the midsummer high light of July, and as I arrived at the site the next day, I thought that it was starting to feel like July, too. In the woods now there were only evanescent glints of sun and the full-grown maple leaves looked like stars. Over the valley, the two osprey were doing a courtship flight, with one bird low and one doing a dancing tremolo of wings at the very crown of the sky. They kept in touch with one another with mewing sounds.

What happened that morning was scary. The three men were cautious and gentle with each other, and yet at the same time I caught a feeling of energizing anger because this job was almost impossibly difficult and dangerous. Julian moved his tall ladder, jumping, testing. Below us, the pileated woodpecker drummed from a hollow tree somewhere in the meadow, his calls resounding dramatically through the entire bowl of the valley.

As I watched, holding my breath, David and Julian had to walk each truss up two ladders at the kitchen side of house while Paul steadied it from within. A rope was tied to the side window beam in the dining room. Then, by himself, Paul hoisted the truss over the frame and tightrope walked it to centre of house where he planned to build a pile of them on the frame of our bedroom. Not only was this maneuvering extremely tricky, but also it was heavy. Earlier, when I had privately tried to lift one of the trusses, made heavier by a large brace of plywood, I could barely get one end off the ground. Even after a truss was up and over the first storey ceiling wall, it was almost impossibly tough for Paul to manipulate single-handed. That morning all of the men were seriously, caringly helpful with each other.

Lying stretched side-by-side, David and Julian were having to trust the stability of their two long shaking and clattering ladders. As I held my breath watching, the whole valley became a rapping in different pitches. The morning's fear was being echoed by the woodpeckers' territorial taps. Then, miraculously, the first truss was up, safely leaning against braces and David had shifted to helping from inside the structure. "To me, David," Paul called down from his perch high overhead. The driving with framing hammer and spikes resounded, seemingly challenging the woodpeckers.

Meanwhile, there was a new transept in use, a yellow one, used by our plumber, who had showed up to work on the sump and the drain since these needed to be completed before the basement cement was laid the following week. "Plumber's pallor," Paul said genially in greeting, looking at his friend's face, which was not tanned because so much of his work was indoors. He scrambled nimbly down off his long ladder to go over the plans that would be needed.

While the two of them were consulting, I walked down to cut the choking, fast-growing field grass around our baby spruces once again. In some places, this grass was now as tall as I was. Seen from near the road, I thought that the truss setup looked incredibly flimsy to support a roof and resist wind and snow. I knew that it was the force holding it all together that counted, but what we had so far did not look like a credible roof. A heron flew over, legs outstretched behind, looking as questioning as I felt.

In the early afternoon, after a convivial lunch with all of us sitting on the plastic chairs I had set out by big rocks that had been removed from the basement cavity, I finished clearing and piling the thorn trees that grew behind the house. I was trying not to think how difficult the truss work was. Below me I heard the neat rustle of gravel from the plumber, working in the basement, which at last was starting to look a little like part of a home. On the site, the breeze had dropped now, leaving the air more humid. A female oriole flashed by. From the forest of trusses I heard, "An eighth of an inch in back. It might want to go over to you."

For today, the men decided to work an extra hour. A solitary red-tail was calling "keer, keer" in the valley. It was three now — the arsenic hour, the dangerous time when people just want to finish, to get the bloody thing over with. At this point they had shifted to the higher end of the house where they would have to walk the four remaining trusses up. As they tried to set the long ladders in the shifting gravel, there was a palpable mix of fear and weariness. "Dangerous as hell," Paul blurted, as they struggled with it. Now the instructions were curt. I wasn't sure whether they even had a plan for erecting the last trusses, the most difficult ones of all to fit. No longer caring whether I could hear, everyone was muttering a constant riff of "Fuck." There. The outside truss at the back was safely on. This was actually accomplished from the inside, using the scaffolding for support. "Fit to one eighth." I could hear the satisfaction. Now they only had one more to squeeze in, but this last truss could present a "bit of a nailing problem."

A solitary turkey vulture went shooting across the valley on a wind current, or "acrost" as the men had taken to saying in their never-ending play on words. Lean, black-garbed Julian grappled with the ladder he had raised to get Paul off the roof. There, the last patch of plywood was being nail-gunned down on the trusses. Nimbly, Paul tiptoed back across the roof to whack a few more nails into a board. And there he was, leaping neatly back on the ground from the third rung of the ladder.

So far, there were only the slightest stirrings of breeze in the very tops of the surrounding aspens. Later the day's heat and humidity might get to me, but right then I was rejoicing in summer, remembering my happy drive over, when I had passed both rippling hayfields and cut hay. And then, as I made the final turns, I had been dazzled all over again by what would be our shining, dancing lake.

What we had now for a house was a box of varying plywoods: a box that looked (but wasn't) higher than it was long. There remained a few openings that I didn't understand, though they were undeniably useful for passing things through, and perhaps provided light, too. Although I greatly missed being at home writing, I couldn't imagine staying away from the exciting, disruptive, rewarding house-building circus. It was seeming to me that the house-building process was not going fast enough, but also that it was going way too fast.

As I peeked through the as-yet unenclosed opening at the southern patio end, the house interior was a small forest of timbers. Looking at the jumble, I thought it would be a wonder if there was any room left for any of our things in there. "What a great day. It's starting out to be another gorgeous day in the neighbourhood."

Over my head, Paul was keeping going by trilling Mr. Rogers nonsense to himself. Then he shifted gears, muttering to himself about his other clients: "Jane's so stressed she's sick. While Mark, well, Mark is resigned. If it's not painted that's OK, he says. But Jane's stomach is churning. Their house is for sale. What if the new place isn't ready on time? That's what they want to know." He turned back to scrutinize his joints and, pulling himself up to the mark, muttered: "Pretty close isn't going to do it. If it's out half an inch, a quarter of an inch, it just isn't going to do it."

"The ramp of death," said Paul, clowning as David and Julian wheelbarrowed plywood up into the house. Quite quickly several sheets of plywood were nailed on overhead, with Paul explaining to me that he wanted to secure at least one side of the roof that day. Until the flimsy roof structure could be held together with the plywood sheathing, an east or west wind in a storm could easily blow the structure over.

Today's delivery seemed disarranged. Since there were no eight-inch spikes in stock, Ken from the hardware store, who usually was so helpful, had sent ten-inch ones. Worse, he had included the wrong door lock set for the exterior. "Bad Kenny. Kill Kenny," warbled Paul. "Would that be Kilkenny?" David rapped back, thinking longingly of icy beer. Now Paul apologized to the delivery man for returning the unneeded cement he had ordered in case Terry didn't arrive in time. "Tell Kenny I'll buy him a beer the next time I see him in a bar."

"That'll be a bar in Harlem," quipped David, referring to a nearby hamlet, which definitely did not have a bar.

Black and white admiral butterflies flittered everywhere in the hot sun.

"Which way do you want to go?" Paul asked Julian of the two by four he was thrusting upwards. "To me?"

After lunch the men were back on the roof. What had begun looking simple, at least to me, now looked a good deal more complicated, with blocks supporting the bases of the trusses too. This was turning into a sticky, breathless day when everything irritated me — the grinding noise of the running generator, the messy dirt piles, the open septic pit and house foundation, the scar of the hydro trench, and the mud pile at the side of the driveway. Everything. Trying to shake my mood, I walked over to the back meadow by the ironwood forest. Even in this listless, suffocating weather the field was alive with brilliant orange hawkweed, as glowingly beautiful as I remembered it to be last summer.

As the process moved on, one morning on the car radio on the drive over, I heard prize-winning Canadian author Isobel Huggan saying that if she'd known how well the past five years would go for her, she wouldn't have worried about anything. I needed to turn my thoughts that way. For example, the previous day, I had rented a sixteen-foot truck, which David drove, and we had gone to Kingston to pick up our windows. After watching how deftly he had backed the balky truck neatly between two piles of glass windows outside the warehouse loading dock I had exclaimed. "I don't know how you can do that!"

"It's mainly trust," he had replied humbly. That morning, as I thought about this I was remembering the anxious time when our three workmen were working on the trusses. The builders' very lives depended on each other. Paul, for instance, had to count on Julian setting the ladder up safely. As any site manager knew, trust is not licence. But, I reminded myself, maybe I needed to be more trusting more of the time. Certainly one couldn't build a large, expensive structure like a house without it.

I sat off to one side, watching the house closing in before my eyes as the men finished covering the roof structure with plywood. When we were talking that morning, Paul had said "roof on today, windows tomorrow." Before they went away for their month of work elsewhere, he told me that the roof would be shingled, and all would be locked up tight. The red-tails were calling piercingly from the valley.

"Hurry David, it's going to rain." There was a big gusting wind, and dark clouds were rushing in. Paul, red-capped and turquoiseshirted, was at the very peak of the roof at the high, bedroom end. Only a few more sheets of plywood were needed to finish covering the roof. "Thwack, thwack, thwack" went the nail gun. "It'll get even stronger with every bit of stuff we put on it," David had told me this morning when I said how surprised I was by its new sturdiness.

As I watched, the clouds passed, and after the brief burst of cold it was warm and muggy again. From where I sat, surrounded by yellow hawkweeds and waist-high green grass, I could feel the afternoon's weather turning and turning. Meanwhile, I was hugging to myself the memory of a secret pleasure. Yesterday morning, the workmen's day away, timid as I am about heights, I had managed to walk up the daunting, tippy gangplank to peek into our shell of a house. Already I could tell how comfortable and safe and well-built our home would be, and even sheathed as the frame was now, I got inklings of how pleasing it would be.

The following morning, with last night's rain still dripping off trees, at the site all was wet, and once again the slick clay was making getting around difficult. There was just no way to get free of the muck. Although I arrived feeling draggy and glum, this turned out to be one of the high point days: one I would not have wanted to miss. Suddenly, the building was moving ahead quickly. Already a significant number of holes for the windows had been cut out, and more were being cut all the time. We had placed our order for these windows long ago in January. Now, it was magical to see what we'd planned for, waited for, come to life. As if they were simply opening a door, Paul and Julian pulled out the chipboard where the dining room double window was to be inserted, letting in much light and giving a whole new broad view. Why, looking at these promising new gaps, it appeared to me that the house was almost all windows. I stuffed my notebook back in my yellow canvas rucksack and ran around to watch my wished-for hall window being cut out. The funny thing was that the new windows felt just as I dreamed they would, only more so.

Because I had forgotten to bring my sandwich lunch, I had intended to leave the site early and go home, but instead I became so interested in watching the work that I stayed on. Even the dining room window, the hardest and heaviest of all the windows, was now well fitted, and Paul was securing it by screwing in many, many carefully chosen screws. From there he would go on to levelling and caulking the windows and then to the tricky fitting and hanging of the front door. When I looked at the outside of the house, I liked the general symmetry that had come about, although this impression was not something that I had planned.

Saturday, we went to check an exceptional sale of remaindered flowers, trees, and shrubs. Admittedly a lot of these were in wretched shape, but we did find some excellent plants. I bought a rich pink *John Davis* rose and a snowy white *Henry Hudson* and a healthy box plant, something I've always wanted to try, as well as a cardinal flower to grow beside our little pond. I added them to the holding bed along the valley down in the meadow, along with the birds' nest spruce, the dark purple butterfly bush, and the silver spotted pulmonaria, which I had bought earlier. While I was digging them in, I found a fresh, bright turkey feather. Other than the wail of distant trains crossing north of us and a passing ATV, it was very quiet there, grey and damp before the evening's promised rain.

Starting in July, Paul planned to be away for a month doing a couple of outside jobs for other customers as we had agreed when we signed the contract. While he was working elsewhere, as site managers we technically were responsible for coordinating the trades. This would mean we would have three big projects to get through: plumbing, hydro, and heating and cooling. After talking with him about what July would bring, Barry and I went down in the valley to continue clipping and clearing brush. In the dense island at the bottom of the Deer Run, Barry was charmed to find a

splendid large toad, and he brought it for me to admire. Further
down the valley in the leafy forest overstorey, alerted by scolding
calls of blue jays I discovered what I thought was a short-eared owl.
Eventually we drove home tired but full of self-congratulatory
accomplishment, basking in the feeling that we were getting
somewhere, that the end was, distantly, in sight.

That very evening, we were drawn back over to the land to see
the almost full moon. As if we were two ghosts looking in on our
beloved land, hand-in-hand we walked down the dim driveway.
Eager to get to the meadow while the thrushes were still calling, for
once we hurried past the house. Very high, the golden, haloed moon
floated above the great pine on the crest of the ridge. At our feet the
flowery field grasses stirred ever so slightly in the air. The great
trees sheltering the valley had a mystery to them, as if they too were
preparing to rest, drawing their leaves about them. The rich, sweet
perfume of the flowering milkweeds surrounded us. Besides loving
my family and friends, this passionate love of the land was the only
sureness I would have in life. In this alone could I rest. I wanted to
live with it every minute that was given to me. We wandered on to
the pond, listening to the chuckle of the leaping spring water
rippling over the rock.

Eventually we returned from the valley to look at our house-to-
be. By now, surrounded by woods, in spite of the moon it was
getting quite dark. While Barry investigated the basement and
climbed up the tall ladder to check the rooms, I knew it was too dark
for me to try this, so I turned instead to one of my favourite spots,
between The Glade and the living room, looking in the newly placed
windows as best I could. And wonderfully, in the dooryard ash tree
a wood thrush burst into loud song right beside me, and continued
boldly in spite of my presence. Before we left we drove down to the
end of the road in the dimness. And sure enough, there now were
lights in the newly finished house there. Our first neighbours had
moved in.

I began my next day at the site laughing in a sunshower. The previous night we had received a call to let us know that our three inches of basement cement would be poured the next day. Amazingly, by the time I arrived at nine-thirty the men were nearly finished the pouring and mixing and levelling. What a sight it was in the dim, open basement cavern. The workmen had rigged one floodlight to the ceiling, but it didn't shed much light. Six naked-to-the-waist labourers were skillfully and quickly working the cement that was being poured in through a tube inserted in the laundry room window. One was levelling the soupy mixture by sweeping a broad board with two handles attached to it; one was wheelbarrowing cement back and forth, while the others were slogging gravel with shovels. Within the house itself, our builders were working zealously. Paul had returned for the day and I could hear him giving loud, clear orders that carried over the machine noises.

Meanwhile, as I sat in the middle of The Glade, a freshening wind was releasing tiny sparkling showers of rain from the trees as weather blew off into a sunny and beautifully clear morning. Happily solitary, I was savouring the high, open shade, the gleams of sun on the woodland grass, the sweet rush of wind in the trees, the delicious woodland coolness on a hottish day, the call of the nesting redwings and the exquisite song sparrow.

All kinds of possibilities were opening up. We were coming into the sweet time now, the reward for so much hard work. The building these days felt like a party. I had learned to like being asked, "Do you want?" or "Would you rather?". Almost every day now brought new gifts, the greatest of which was my ongoing exploration of this piece of land.

After an hour working on my notes, I stretched and wandered down to the new path I had cut through the meadow, moving in the heat through the dance of the rich, ripening grass, feeling the spirit rising. In my holding garden it pleased me to see that the buddleia now was blooming, a lovely rich colour, somewhere between azure and violet. I ate my quick lunch—hardboiled egg, olives, and sourdough bread—with great relish down there, enjoying the treasures waiting to be set around a completed house. Then, since the cement man had not returned to run his setting machine over the concrete, I decided to go farther and visit the lake. On this changeable day, the sky had completely clouded over again, softening to a waiting-for-rain greyness. Protected by my rubber boots, I splashed through the shallow, sandy-bottomed lake out to a fallen tree. For fifteen minutes I sat on this, feeling part of the lake, watching the small waves, running my eye over the lovely lines of driftwood, and listening to the holiday sounds of gulls, along with that of a wren trilling across the bay. Finally, I pulled myself up and walked slowly and appreciatively past a little hill dense with the rich blue of the unfortunately named Viper's Bugloss, crossed the road and followed the cart track and the Deer Run home. Arriving back at the house, I was in time to watch the last remaining workman starting his long afternoon of hoovering his machine back and forth over our new basement floor, patiently setting the new concrete.

VIII

Coming Along Quickly

Things were coming along very quickly now. I got a call to let me know that an Ontario Hydro crew would come some time in the next week to hook us into the grid. Having electricity would mean that the electrician could start wiring, so Barry arranged for him to come the following Monday. After that, it turned out that the heating and cooling men also would arrive to start roughing in.

Although I was struggling with a cold, which made me feel tired and dizzy, we drove over to the house, feeling it would be our best chance to decide the locations of outlets and vents before the electrician and duct specialists arrived the next week. Unfortunately, this meant that I absolutely had to climb the dreaded tall ladder, in spite of my fear that I might choke completely halfway up it. Barry was sympathetic, but inflexibly determined that I was going to get up to the main floor to see all the progress. Now that it was sufficiently cured, for the first time we could walk across the fine, smooth basement concrete, and I tried out the ladder Paul had left there leading from the basement to the first floor. Heights had been a barrier for me since my many failed childhood attempts to ascend to the intriguing attic above my bedroom. Today, feeling woozy from my cold, I simply couldn't see how I would get up, especially since I would have to dodge the provisional safety railing the men had hammered on at the top of the stair well. Stalling, I suggested that maybe it would be easier to go up by way of the front door. So, patiently Barry fetched the longer ladder from behind the house and set it up in the narrow gravelled trench at the front. Because of the trench that surrounded the house, the ladder had to be almost vertical, which made it all the more tippy. To my shaky feet, the mud-clogged rungs seemed narrow and irregularly spaced. Inevitably, halfway up, I reached a rung where I felt too high. Amazingly, though, Barry's encouragement and my determination pulled me up. With a hidden sob of fear, I easily crawled off the high ladder and onto the plywood floor. Dazzling. This was my first time within the framed space, with all the windows mounted in place. My first impression, besides the light and airiness, was that the surprising height of our first floor above ground gave it a treehouse feeling. Slowly, we paced round all the rooms, planning, and then I spent more time by myself simply appreciating.

"You'll be pleased when I'm done," Paul had told us at our meeting in January. And yes, I was infinitely pleased. After I eased back down the ladder, I paused for a moment to study our house from the outside with satisfaction. The soft, unobtrusive grey-black shingles, for instance, gave exactly the look I'd hoped for. I could see the house fitting its site neatly and vanishing into the clearing, just as we had hoped it would. Cottagey, simple, and a bit idiosyncratic: that was the feeling I was wishing for.

The following Monday was another of the exceptional days when many things came together at once. Fortunately Barry was able to come with me that day, and we arrived before eight, pleased to find that Paul and his crew had not left us to deal with all this on our own. Now that their main focus was another job elsewhere, we had not been sure whether they would be able to come. Feeling beatific surveying the work from this vantage point, I sat on the entrance hall floor beside the open stairwell, looking down into a basement floored with beautifully smooth cement, watching David and Julian making our stairs. The construction of these stairs was a bonus, which I hadn't expected to happen for some time. By the time we arrived, they had three riser boards laid out with a couple of treads to hold the structure together, and they had also made the turn-around platform that was to go at the bottom. There. Paul joined them, and all three men just hoisted the whole stair frame up and matched it with the ceiling and the platform. Very quickly, they screwed on the rest of the treads. So exciting.

Behind me on the first floor, John, the electrician, was methodically setting up for work. It being summer holiday time, his seventeen-year-old son Lucas had come with him to help screw boxes into the wall and to fetch and carry. Father and son had an easy, affectionate relationship. As soon as they were ready, Barry and I went around with John, who was intense and worked swiftly, deciding the locations of plugs and switches. It turned out that the switches for our design of house would be difficult to place, what with the layout of kitchen cabinets, the fridge placement, pantry and the open concept in general.

We were barely started when the heating and cooling men arrived to do their preliminary layout. At this point we had to separate, with Barry going downstairs to do chimney and basement planning with them while I carried on working with John on the wiring plans. How satisfying to be able to improvise and change locations including useful places for phone and computer jacks so easily and quickly. When John and I were almost done our planning, three huge hydro trucks showed up to connect us. Everything was converging on this one day. Meanwhile, adding to the bustle in driveway, the hardware truck arrived to deliver more lumber. Through the open front door I saw Barry and David alternating, carrying this wood around the back where it would be stored.

As if there wasn't enough going on, when I walked down the hall to check the location of a switch, I glanced out my cherished casement window and caught sight of Terry's helper, Eddie, preparing to fill in our septic bed with a small digger. Then, at eleven the generator went silent. We were connected to electricity at last!

A few days later, I felt as if I was in the midst of chaos at the site. Now that we had power someone had a radio on, which added a sense of canned cheer to a day when the weather was grey, heavy, and still. Much as I detested the machine noises that underlaid the radio, at least they felt like a necessary part of progress. John had set up a metal bar holding numerous spools of electrical wire to be fed to the various outlets around the upstairs, and the cavernous upstairs interior already was festooned with an orderly disarray of wires. Today we actually had four electricians working on this puzzle: John and his son Lucas, plus two more.

Of course, there was a lot of banter. As well as working diligently himself, John was also orchestrating, checking, and teaching his apprentices. There was a lot of discussion about whether screws were better than spikes, about the braiding of wires, and about how a new television workshop had recommended electrical tape rather than staples for securing wire to the two-by-fours. Someone mentioned deer: "I hate those stupid forest rats," but then, inexplicably, went on to say, "Of course I'm from Wolfe Island." In the dark basement utility room, the heating and cooling crew had set up a table and a trouble lamp and were doing expert, complicated-looking work shaping metal ducts.

Today's construction noises were truly hellacious. As well as the big reciprocating saw, a very long drill shook the house. I had brought a chair to practice looking at views, considering the use and feel of rooms, and that turned out to be the best thing I could have done to help myself feel at home with the new space. After that, I fanned out sample paint and floor colours to consider, and then, for the first time I went down to the basement by our newly made stairs. On that day, I could see how this organism, our house-to-be, sustained the momentum of defining itself. As for the decisions, we were chipping away at them, coming closer all the time.

But actually, today there were enough people working that there was nowhere I could lurk for long without being in someone's way. From time to time I caught sight of my friends the robins, flopping distressed from the nearby woods to the dirt pile to my brush piles. It seemed that the changing landscape troubled them more than the truly frightful noises.

Then Tuesday, after all the workmen had left for the day, we came over with our visiting friends, Umberto and Judy, and started to do some actual living there. That day, sitting together with them in great conviviality on four rickety green plastic chairs arranged on the plywood floor in the living room was something we would never forget. This was the first time we had actually sat down with friends in our house, and already we were feeling at home. Having just decorated her own home, Judy had good ideas such as using a single paint colour to tie in the whole open part of the house, while Bert suggested various small design improvements, based on his own recent experience of building their own house. Sitting together around what would be our hearth was very cheering, a promise of pleasant times ahead, and we felt cherished and affirmed. When we got home I asked Barry to spread out our new crimson Kilim rug in the living room and then I spilled paint chips all over it, and the four of us played at choosing the best colour combinations.

A few days later, after our friends left for home, we drove over to the land on our own, where we were pleased to find a young local farmer rolling the swathes of raked golden, fragrant hay neatly into round muffin bales as he had promised us that he would. With Molly dashing before us on her short dachshund legs, we had a blissful walk the full length of the newly cleared fields.

As promised, our builders returned at the beginning of August. Over the past month while they were elsewhere, I had been surprised to find that I felt less lonely when I was at our house site by myself than when the place was full of workmen. Nevertheless, it was cheering to see our house under way once more. Today all the men were energized and ready to push ahead, and I was pleased by their progress. Paul's newly installed shallow grey tile floor pad for the woodstove was as handsome as we had hoped it would be, and unlike other raised floor pads, it made a smooth transition to the rest of the living room. Not only was I starting to see the end in sight, but I knew there would be some sweet times ahead—seeing the woodstove delivered and placed on the grey tiles, for instance, but also the kitchen cupboards that we had chosen last winter would be installed, and we would get our first look at the walls painted in the colours we had chosen.

The following Sunday, Barry and I sat at our farm kitchen table making lists of questions for the plumber and the electrician, and for Terry and Paul, along with many notes for ourselves. Then at night we had a meeting with Terry in an attempt to move through a procedural blockage. While Paul was saying that progress was stalled because of Terry's failure to install the required O-ring around the footings, Terry was insisting that the outside vapour barrier needed to be laid before he could place the O-ring. Meanwhile, the heating and cooling company representative had warned us that his men wouldn't be able to finish their basement installation until the footings had been filled in. Although our meeting with Terry didn't move us ahead far on most of our questions, we did achieve a fairly firm promise that he would put in the O-ring before the week was over.

After we finished discussing logistics, Terry stayed a while to visit, telling stories of the wild ways people spend money. Take, for example, a woman client who said to him, "I know you guys all cheat. Don't even think of talking to me about money. Just tell me how much and I'll keep the cheques coming." Another woman, and privately I asked myself why so many of these stories were about women, watched Terry's men do extensive blasting into a rocky site for her foundation, only to tell him she thought she'd prefer the house switched in a different direction. "Lady, it's not a boat!" he protested. "We can't just turn it around to suit you." I told him that talking to one of the neighbours in the area, I also had been shocked by some of the casual attitudes about expenses. Talking about her new cottage, she had looked me straight in the eye and actually said, "You know, if I want it, I *have* to have it!"

A week later, when we finally found time to drive over to the site again, I met an exhausted David just packing to leave. He told us curtly that the missing sheets of drywall that had been holding up the builders had finally been delivered. Throwing his tools into the trunk of his car, he remarked that insulating a ceiling was stifling, miserable work, and, not surprisingly, drywalling was another job everyone disliked.

The low, cool light gave a September feeling to the afternoon. Like David, I too was feeling drained and edgy, and this meant that once again doubts surfaced. People had told us that the house would seem larger after the drywall was up. It didn't. After the wonderful airy feeling of open ceilings and windows viewed through the framing I actually felt slightly claustrophobic inside the house. What if we had made a mistake? What if we wouldn't be able to make this new house work for us? What if we felt too alone living here? What if we came to hate this place into which we had poured so much effort and love?

That night, back at the park, still panicking, after supper I dragged out the paint samples to consider them one more time. And finally, amazingly, the decisions became clear and straightforward. Patient visiting and revisiting the design process worked for me every time. If only I could remember that. We had colours that I believed would make us happy—an unusual complex light pea green which has both blue and yellow casts in it, a goldenrod yellow to make the living room look like a glowing cave set apart from the rest of the house, and the rich Tuscan pink-brown, a heart colour, for my writing room and the guest room.

Friday morning I wrote out these colours and drew maps for Paul of where each one should go while Barry calculated the amounts needed. Then we made a list of the light fixtures we had and those we still needed to buy. When I scurried over briefly at noon to deliver the paint list to Paul so he could pick it up on the weekend, I found that much of the drywalling was done and that Paul and "the boys" were packing up the impressive ceiling drywall machine to return. They should finish putting up the walls on Monday, they told me, and then it would be on to applying the siding. When I offered the usual wishes for a good weekend, tired as they were, they looked as if that possibility was beyond consideration.

After the men drove off, I stood staring at a single sweet pink rose that I had discovered on one of the bushes in the small holding bed we had established down in the valley. What with the ongoing packing and calling for moving estimates, I too was simply thankful that this heavy week was nearly over. Recently, Paul had taken to wearing a small brace on his right arm. I was thoroughly sick of the whole process, including the occasionally body-straining demands on the fine men making our home. Yes, if the builders weren't working for us, they would be doing the same kinds of work for someone else. Still, the crew had been the best of people to have, patient, kind, and helpful, and it troubled me to be an agent in this wear. In fact, I now had reached the point where I'd rather not even go near the house.

Trying to regain the feeling of our early times visiting the land, that Sunday I suggested to Barry that we bring a picnic supper and sit in the beautiful newly-mown back bay, and then go for a walk through the hilly fields that wound to the north of our property. We wouldn't go to see the house, I promised him. Surprisingly, he acquiesced gladly. I whipped together sausages, tiny noodles with fresh tomato and onion sauce, and market broccoli, and ladled the hot food into our old familiar red enamel casserole, the one we always used for travelling. The sky had clouded and it was actually cold, but we did enjoy our picnic, one of the few festive attempts of the summer. Then Barry had an inspiration, suggesting that we drive around and come to the cartway from the far end so we could see the land from the viewpoint where we first discovered it almost exactly two years ago. Standing looking at the valley opening out before us, backed by the wall of trees at the far end, gladness welled in us again.

But after we arrived back home, I couldn't help getting witchy-waily with worries once again. After thirty years, our move would be such a big change for us. We weren't used to neighbours. What if bad neighbours spoiled our solitude? What would I do if there was a fire that extinguished the trees? On this anguished evening when I was so heart-weary, I felt the bitter reality that with every step we were taking we were tearing the strands of long experience and love that bound us to life at Foley Mountain. That fall we would be shifting our allegiance once again as we did in our early years together when we had made six moves in six years, although this time, at last, it would be to our very own place. That night I was acutely aware of the commitment of love and hope I was making to Singing Meadow and, as with all love, how very risky that was.

The next week I popped over to see Lloyd, a remarkable man whom Barry was fond of calling "the world's oldest plasterer." Although it was another dim day, thanks to the light thrown by Lloyd's floodlamps, the bedroom where he was working looked cheeringly bright and roomlike. Still working at almost seventy-five, Lloyd looked and sounded plastery when he talked. He was white all over, with a white that I doubted ever came off, and even his voice was whispery. Lloyd had worked for us before at the park house, and I knew he took pride in doing a careful job.

He had always been gallant, but that morning he hurt my feelings by mumbling "I prefer old houses myself." In many ways I agreed and I told him that an old house was what we'd originally hoped to have, before we discovered we couldn't get any land we liked. Since he didn't budge, unwisely I pressed on: "Oh well, at least we won't have to worry about upkeep."

"But that's part of the fun," he retorted, not letting me off the hook.

IX

The Last Big Push

After a surprising cold night, it was another radiant morning. We were surrounded by rushes of breeze, and everywhere the play of light and green was enchanting. An early, tentative cicada called. Both of us were waiting for Terry to come one last time to spread topsoil around the house.

Although it would have been a great comfort to begin establishing new beds, by September I had pretty much given up on getting the work done to prepare for these. Knowing that we would have to wait a long three years before we would be able to harvest our own asparagus and rhubarb, easy crops we had enjoyed at the park, it was disappointing to think that we would greet our first spring at Singing Meadow having no gardens whatsoever. Now, though, an autumn drought was setting in. Watering transplants would have been much easier if the outside tap had been hooked to the well, but unfortunately this would not take place until the house was ready for all the final plumbing. Just to water the trees we had planted took me a ridiculous two hours of slogging, carrying buckets from our little pond back in the meadow. At a time when we were so busy, even this much watering was a bad idea. Much as our new trees meant to me, I accepted that if the drought continued I would have to let them die.

Our new home looked like a natural place for gardening. When I first started dreaming I suggested to Barry that we might have fruit trees towards the front of the property. Along our road frontage we would have masses of sunflowers, cosmos, hollyhocks: a gift for people passing on the road. Behind that, in the sunniest area, I wanted a large vegetable garden. Since our first years together, we had always had one of these, working side by side whenever we could, growing and harvesting as much of our food as possible.

In the clearing behind the house site I wanted at least one perennial bed. I'd need a place for wild familiar friends, such as the tall yellow-starred elecampane of August pastures, but also I wanted to include the old-fashioned shrubs I had loved since childhood, the heartening butter yellow of early-flowering forsythia, then, later, the confetti blossoms of bridal wreath and the richly scented creamy white mock orange.

At this stage, though, the reality was that the actual making of gardens was appearing to be difficult. My few forays into digging in the rough, gravelly soil had shown me that I would be unlikely to be able to clear more than a tiny patch. We talked of getting someone to plough the vegetable garden with a tractor, and that was doable. Less sure would be the creation of flower gardens. First of all, the soil we found was skimpy. How much soil could we afford to bring in? Would we even be able to break the soil we already had with a rototiller?

All the same, we still were hoping to make a start on the shade garden that we envisioned stretching in a curving sweep behind our house. But on a Sunday afternoon, after three heavy, tough hours of bull-work, with Barry digging holes and me wheelbarrowing loads from the good rich mounds of soil that Allan had delivered the week before, reality was setting in. Undoubtedly, this heavy digging and wheelbarrowing was not good for either of us. My lack of upper body strength was humbling. Although he still was much stronger than me, Barry, too, was finding the work hard. As I emptied wheelbarrow after wheelbarrow of soil, the nagging fear crept in that maybe we would never be able to create the gardens we wished for.

And then, most wonderfully, there came a rescue. Around three, when we were about to give up, Terry arrived with his digger. He had left his son Justin at one of his properties to cut grass and it ended up being convenient for him to stay nearby rather than drive back and forth he explained. "Do you think you'd have time to help us with this?" Barry clutched his friend's arm and gestured at our pathetic achievements. Cheerfully, kindly, using the small digger, within half an hour he finished shifting soil to the new garden and then, neatly using the bucket of the digger, he made quick work of the rest of the holes, a tremendous boost. Without his help our shade garden would never have happened.

Seeing by his watch that he still had a few minutes, he lingered with us, leaning on the digger. "You're lucky you've got yourselves a builder who orders ahead," he told us. That morning he had heard that the surge of rebuilding after two horrendous Florida hurricanes meant that this fall supplies, including plywood, would either be very expensive or else unobtainable.

After Terry drove off, I stood looking around, feeling a flood of amazement and gratitude that I would have flower gardens after all. The queer thing was that, in spite of my fretting about planning suitable locations for these, in the end, they just evolved. Right from our first visits to the site, I had envisioned clearly the long, curving border in the shade of the maples. This shade garden would be a new adventure for me, a place where I could experiment with ferns and hostas and aruncus. But I knew I also wanted a sunlit flower garden, sheltered behind our house. However, much as I tried, I could not see how to fit another border into the space. But then, one morning recently, Allan unexpectedly rolled up with a dump truck filled with extra topsoil and asked in a hurry, "Where do you want this?" There was no time to consider. "Just make a mound of it, roughly circular would be good, over there in the centre of the clearing," I gestured. And so, with no planning whatsoever we ended with a round perennial garden, which turned out to be an ideal focal point along our wandering path to the Deer Run and the valley beyond. Now that I was seeing the two areas roughed out with spread soil, I thought that I couldn't have chosen better locations.

Ever since childhood I had made gardens. The only way I ever was able to do this was by sticking plants in with little poor preparation, and then over the years I improved the soil in every way I could. "Please forgive me," I said to my much-loved plants. "I know this is not right, but it's all I can manage." For what I imagined would be my last gardens I had meant to do the job right, carefully preparing the ground with double-digging and soil enrichments, but as it turned out, once again my plants would have to make do with a bare minimum of preparation. But now, thanks to Terry and Allan, at least I knew I would have the chance to grow them.

Along our driveway I wanted to have a border with the rugosa roses that were waiting in the holding bed, and also with daylilies, which I would divide from the plants that I grew at the park. But a surprising gift was a makeshift tiny rock garden. As Allan had removed rocks when he dug the foundation, he piled them beyond the septic bed. With bits of soil tucked in, I saw that I could experiment with this, supplementing it with more interesting rocks from the piles scattered around our own land.

It was the end of the first week in September and, after several weeks without rain, the soil was alarmingly powdery and the plants were droopy. Nearby, a tree frog was piping and I was pleased to know that he was there. Rain felt imminent, though, and a heavy wind was rushing through the trees, perhaps the prelude to the approaching tail end of Hurricane Frances.

Then, overnight the hurricane remnants ripped north across the continent, and by morning torrents of rain were beating down in visible lines. My careful drive across country on overflowing roads felt both risky and thrilling. In the violently gusting wind, I strained to watch for fallen limbs and avoided skidding on slick washboarded back roads or hydroplaning on highways awash with racing water. When I reached our new house, I was startled to find a small river flowing down the depression of our filled-in hydro trench and ending in a small pond, which had formed over the foot of our vegetable garden-to-be. Unfortunately this now looked even lower than I had expected.

When I slipped through our front door, noticing what a difference the portable lights made for cheer, ambiance, and even warmth, I found Paul painting ceilings and whistling. The stormy weather would be a good test of this house, he said, sending David out to halt a washout by adding a spare piece to our newly installed eaves-trough drainpipes. Julian was expected to show up for work too, but he had not appeared.

I hadn't wanted to miss this day because, in spite of the fierce storm, our kitchen cupboards were to be delivered, and indeed, at ten, just at coffee break time, a small panel truck pulled up right to the front stairs. While I stood inside comfortably staring out the kitchen window as if through a cascading waterfall, David and Paul hurried out in the beating rain to help unload the packed truck. First they hauled out bulky green insulation bales and heaved them through our front door. Next, they slid out flat panels and then the first of a lot of intriguing tall boxes, stacking all of them in what will be the dining room for now. Working their way up and down the rain-slicked stairs was heavy, awkward work. While I held my breath, they wrestled in a huge box that was labelled as the upper big corner cabinet, and this was followed by two more large ones, which were tugged safely in. The truck had also brought the full-length glass door that would go at the dining room end of our house and I could see that it was beautiful. There. That was the lot. The truck splashed back out the driveway and left us completely isolated in the green, rain-washed world.

"Leave space to get at the walls," David reminded Paul as they sorted piles of boxes. Unfortunately for me, in my eagerness, Paul warned me that the cabinets might not be installed until the following week. And even I had to admit that it made sense for him to finish painting the walls. For the time being I contented myself with peeking through rents to look at the colour, and while the oak I detected was definitely fake, it was a pleasant, grainy shade of fake, I decided.

Even though the rain was blowing past the kitchen window horizontally, inside the house felt solid, and we were muffled from the brunt of the storm. Not a drop of what would turn out to be four inches of rain penetrated the basement. Now that he had returned to painting the back rooms, Paul was singing cheerfully and was whistling, too. Mostly it was quiet downstairs where David was working. It would appear that nothing else significant would happen that day.

But there was Julian, at last, squeaking with excitement as he reported that he was late because the roads he travelled had been actually flooded and even blocked by fallen trees. Closer to Kingston, Perth Road was washed out, he told us. Graders were out trying to repair it. Before he left his apartment, he said, the weather station on TV showed a gigantic red warning mass over Kingston. David added that he had heard that Lanark, Kingston, and Prince Edward Country all were to be badly hit. And yet here we sat in our quiet oasis, barely aware of the great storm.

A few days later, Barry dropped over to check the progress on the house. "After your errands this afternoon, maybe you should go and see what you think," he suggested. And so I did, stepping into the house, which by then was all quiet and tidy after everyone had left. The green we had chosen turned out to be fascinating. "Pea green," I should have said, but its effect was more complex than that. What was special was that it changed significantly in every light. At the end of the hall, it was soft, misty, blue-ish, while in the open kitchen the same colour became assertive, bright, and light. Surprisingly, in actual sunlight it appeared as a yellow green. And then there was the living room's yellow. With the contrasting matte black of the woodstove chimney pipe, the strong goldenrod looked stunning.

Our long-planned vision for the house was certainly coming together. On a recent trip to Kingston for fittings, we had picked up a print of Ansel Adams' *Fiat Lux*, which had jumped out at me from the front of a bin. We both knew that this black-and-white photograph of light through the great redwoods belonged in our

new home. And now, seeing the painted walls, I knew just the place
for it in what would be my writing room.

Back at the park, preparing to leave Foley Mountain was
becoming a wrench I no longer seemed to be able to make myself
perform. Part of this was an unexpectedly weepy hour for me while
I went through my hoard of children's art and discarded much of it.
Although I knew I would feel better once I had taken apart the
trappings of many years, I was almost unable to do so. Our
bookcases, for example, were my particular landmarks. Each time I
passed the tall one in the downstairs hall, which I built myself to fit
this space, the now emptied shelves were a continuing reproach. At
this stage of dismantling, I felt rootless.

Now, at mid-September, the roadside sumacs were half
crimson, as were the red maples near ponds, and the ash leaves had
turned a rich gold. I had come over to deliver the packages of
bathroom and hall tiles that Barry and I had picked up in Kingston
on the weekend. When I drove in, my eyes were caught by the wall
of fine tall sugar maple trees on the far side of our lot. The first
autumn we came here, one of the first things I fell in love with had
been this view of superb, large trees, reminiscent to me of the
grandeur of a European landscape. Meanwhile, a small flight of wild
geese sailed right past the open bedroom window. Down in valley I
heard a raven qwonking.

David stepped away from the swirling eddy of updrafted air
and sparks from a quick fragrant bonfire of lumber and cardboard
packing scraps in the back yard that he had been supervising and
came to help me carry the heavy packages into the house. It turned
out that this was to be the long-awaited cupboard building day.
Already Paul and elegant Julian, in his usual black and with his
impressive tattoos of flames up his arms, had ripped open a number
of boxes. Before the men could actually make a start, this big job
required a lot of preparation. In the kitchen there was much stud
tapping, measuring with levels, and searching out screws with just

the right bite to them. Then Paul brought David in to help Julian shunt the awkward corner cabinet up so he could measure, mark, and put screws directly into the studs. Squeezed between his two men, it was difficult for Paul working up on his ladder. To help the work along there was a background of relentless, hard-driving radio. I was beginning to see that this fitting would be more tense and less fun than I had expected.

Out of his tool chest Paul pulled a beautiful old wood clamp to hold the next cabinet to the first. "One and a half inch screw. I want more aggressive ones," he called out, casting aside the screws the hardware store had supplied and rummaging impatiently through his boxes for saved ones of his own. At this stage, the cabinets were braced adequately, but still minimally. Privately, I thought that already they looked as if they'd always been there, and their warm colouring looked delicious with the soft grey-green walls.

The day before, Sunday, we had dug up all the plants I was moving, maybe sixty of them. Although I was careful to leave part of every plant for the new tenants of the park house, as I drove my spade into the hearts of plants and tore them apart I felt I was destroying what I had built over so many years. Without Barry's strength and understanding, I would never have been able to do this.

Now, after I worked through all the day's questions with Paul while he was on his coffee break, I spent three and a half hours on my own, beginning the heavy work of setting up the new shade gardens here where Terry had helped prepare the bed.

After all the men had left for the day, and I had finished my planting, I groped my way to the tiny stream bordering our property to wash my hands. Sheltered in tall field grass, I sat there watching the low sun flickering on the stream and trees, renewing my strength to go back to the job. From the nearest bay of the lake, there were the joyous calls of many migrant geese, who would rest there overnight. If I was to get through this process, I knew I must hold onto such things.

Later, before I left, I treated myself to wandering through the house, getting used to the dusky Italian pink walls of my writing room to be, which seemed very pink just then. After that I went to sit on the floor by the long casement window at the end of the hall, watching remnant sparks from the morning's bonfire flying past. There was such a good, airy feeling to this house.

Saturday Barry dropped me off in Westport to walk around doing errands. Unexpectedly, this ordinary trip turned into a time of love and blessings. It seemed that many knew we would be leaving the park in less than a month and wanted to wish us well. First I slipped into The Salmon House to make sure John, one of the owners, still planned on delivering our winter's firewood. We had a warm and convivial time talking about wood heat. Then I walked over to The Wordsmith to rent a movie. Doug, the owner, was softened, friendly. We would be neighbours at our new place, he pointed out. Over at the pharmacy, Brenda, the owner, and Dorothy, her assistant, were sympathetic and encouraging about Barry retiring. Walking around the corner, I stopped in at Murphy's to pick up our weekend papers. Betty Ann, the owner, told me that although I was rarely the one to come in, she felt that we had a shared friendship because Barry had been such a part of Westport for so many years. Finally done, I sat down to wait for Barry on the bench across the road in front of the hardware store. Here our friend Jack LaPointe joined me, talking sympathetically about our new house. By the time Barry came by to pick me up, I felt gathered in good wishes, and thankful that we will continue to live near this special small village.

At this stage, engaged as I was in preparing to leave the conservation area within weeks, I was relieved not to be at the house site so often. Glancing around the park house, at last I felt a watershed. Enough had been accomplished that I could see that we would get done, and we would get moved. Instead of hating the mounting ugly piles of boxes and the hollow echo of the rooms as we stripped them, I began to think that I was tucking up goodness for my new home. Every box moved us closer. Could it be that time would be given me to create another paradise?

A few days before, at the end of September, we had met with Paul so he could take us over the house and show us what he expected to be able to finish before he left, and we were happy with this. Now, here I was, sitting on our new bedroom floor, with a stream of pale sun coming in the low-silled window. The leaves surrounding the house were beginning to turn, and the reflected warm yellows and oranges glowed against the paint colours. As I had hoped they would, the big windows brought the outdoors in. Just in front of me, I caught a glimpse of a flash of red. There was a pileated woodpecker sending chips flying from the trunk of one of the nearby aspens, which now had lemon-coloured leaves.

Although it already was one o'clock in the afternoon, this was the day on which many things had been promised to happen. But at that point I was completely alone in our almost-finished house, waiting for someone to show up. For the first time. I went over the day's schedule in my mind. Because our move was booked for a Wednesday and Thursday only two weeks away, timing was difficult. Each element depended on the other. Because we were down to our last days, it was crucial that we have all three appliances in place right away. The electrical inspector was booked to come the following Tuesday, and he had to approve the installed dishwasher. In order for the building inspector to sign our final occupancy permit, we must have this electrical approval complete.

Another requisite before we could secure the building inspector's sign-off was that the groundwork must be completed, including covering the septic system and sloping the final soil away from the house to protect the basement from pooling water. As yet, Terry Martin had not come over to finish these jobs. And, as if this was not enough, the cast iron woodstove that was to be our main source of heat was to be delivered.

Because I expected to be busy all day, I brought no reading or knitting with me for a distraction. In case the newly hooked-up phone might ring, I could not even step away from the house. As the light wind changed direction, the sky was greying over with mares' tails. Dreamlike milkweed fluffies were flying high. I hurried out to the car for a moment to fetch our two ratty but friendly old car blankets. These I made into a pad, and lay in our bedroom, gazing at the lovely aspens and maples right outside the windows there. As I waited, though, being alone began to feel more like being lonely.

But very shortly, in an extraordinary burst of activity everything began happening at once. First Terry Martin arrived with his new dump truck and two spreaders. Very quickly he was followed by Allan and a very sunburned Eddie. Soon two diggers were cruising around the house. Looking out the kitchen window at our driveway, I saw Terry himself spreading loads of fine gravel to cover the coarser foundation layer. All over again I was impressed by how much the men and their equipment could get done and how quickly. Already the newly-covered septic area looked greatly better and, for the first time, I could see the land outside my windows looking like a real place, not a building site mounded with dirt. The smell of the many cigarettes that kept the men going was drifting in the open front door.

At four the appliance delivery truck rattled up the driveway, and within minutes the three big boxes were set neatly in the kitchen and the much-watched-for truck was gone. No sooner had this truck swayed back down the driveway, dodging the heavy equipment working there, than Jim Archambault pulled up in his Hearth and Home van. Relishing this better-than-Christmas moment, I hovered, appreciating Jim's pride in the woodstove he skillfully set up for us.

The black matte stove fit like a charm on the grey slate fireplace tiles. Contrasted with the goldenrod-coloured living room walls and the gorgeous autumn colours through the windows, even unlit, it already felt like the heart of our house, just as we had hoped it would.

Surprisingly, in the midst of the turmoil of moving, we were able to redeem Thanksgiving. On the holiday Saturday we came to our new house at four and lit our first of the required three little breaking-in fires. Seeing flames leap for the first time behind the woodstove window felt both sacred and comforting. Leaving the house, we drove to have Thanksgiving dinner at nearby Nordlaw Lodge. In the dining room, with its fine view over the lake, we watched the sun come flaring out against a stark sky and richly coloured fall leaves, only to recede quickly over the dark waters of the lake. Turning to the generous buffet, we had choices of turkey, ham, mashed potatoes, spiced squash, cole slaw, corn, cranberries, chili sauce, gravy, soup, a selection of desserts, wine, and coffee. Because nearly everything now was packed in the kitchen back at home, without Nordlaw, we would have had a poor dinner indeed. Instead, this interlude with the kind owners and cheerful food took us away from our anxieties.

When I drove over to check at Singing Meadow after the weekend, surrounded by beautiful fall colours, I was surprised to see that, because it was mostly clad in late-turning oaks, the great ridge beyond the valley as yet remained unchanged. Still, what this meant was that we would get a second autumn later when the oak leaves finally turned scarlet and rust.

Aware that we were approaching the end of the building process, I stood in the kitchen at a respectful distance, watching Paul, who was making his final adjustments, or "fine tuning the counter," as he described it. Reminding me of a surgeon, he was testing, pushing back and forth, doing lots of finagling with wooden braces under the counter, tapping down with his knife, then patiently loosening off a bolt underneath. Soon, I thought with regret, I would not have his careful work to observe.

X

Harvest

Higgledy-piggledy we were scurrying to the end of house building and our move. The park house was a maze of boxes. Jeremy's former bedroom was ceiling to floor with them. Meanwhile, I pressed ahead, working on the most fidgetty, time-consuming jobs, feeling swamped by logistics. No chore was simple any more. For instance, when I made leek soup with wonderful fat leeks dug from our kitchen garden beside the back porch, I was thwarted when I realized that I'd already packed the food processor blade. The move was taking a toll on our animals, too. They hated the boxes and all of the upheaval, but were most distressed when I worked beneath them in the basement. As I dug through workbench tools to pack, I heard Molly ceaselessly trotting back and forth overhead.

Back at our new house again, I caught up with Terry Martin, who had his son Justin with him. The driveway culvert was in, he told me, and they were just finishing. The mounds that had obstructed our views of the valley since spring were completely gone now, in time for us to see the height of the autumn colour. Fine gravel had been spread, leading to both doors. Especially satisfying was the elegant placement of the handsome large boulders, which Terry and Allan had drawn from our foundation hole in the first days of work. As always, I felt encouraged by his friendliness and enjoyed his obvious pride in the son who was following him in his work.

After Barry's class left, together with Molly, we returned to the new house to check everything one last time. We lit our second breaking-in fire, and watched it blaze up handsomely. After that we went for a restorative ramble back to the five big flaming maples near our little stone wall. A great walker in spite of her tiny size, Molly kept up easily.

It was October fifteenth, and closing day at last. And it happened that this was also the day that great flocks of migrant robins arrived at the berry-laden red cedars of Foley Mountain, more this year than I could ever recall. Before I started my morning's work of packing, I went for a walk. The surrounding fields at the park house were full of not just many, many robins, but also families of nuthatches, chickadees, and sparrows. I even heard one precious white-throated sparrow.

Perhaps fortunately, Barry had the distraction of teaching that morning. After all, there would be little point in our being over at the new house before the afternoon when Paul was finishing. All fall the teaching, with the kind appreciation of so many teachers and the pleasure of working with children, had been both a blessing for him and an obstruction at a time when he needed to give his full attention to the house-building and move.

While he was out teaching a pond study with an eager class of grade threes, I finished clearing the basement, finding some good surprises, such as some misplaced Christmas presents and useful shelf braces, and resolutely pitched into the garbage some very old dog collars that had been saved from long-dead friends.

When we pulled up to the house, I saw that almost everything had been finished as promised. Today, Paul was flying at enclosing the pantry with pine panelling. Superfluous in the midst of the activity, I looked slowly around me, noticing the sawdust smells one last time, hearing the neat popping sounds of the nail gun and the air pig.

The building inspector arrived. On this important day, he was genial, giving us the welcome news that we now were permitted to move in. Although none of us had agreed entirely with everything he wanted, he had been helpful and we felt he had been watching over our project, wanting what he saw as best for us. As we stood talking one last time in the hall, he encouraged us to build a screened porch later and even offered to draw up an acceptable plan for this.

What a strange, otherworldly end to the house building. As early twilight gathered on the dim, rainy afternoon, Paul moved faster and faster. As the sober sky darkened and the time flew past on the newly set dial of the stove clock, all I could do was meekly watch. Unable to cope with this closing frenzy, Barry slipped downstairs to sweep sawdust. Standing mouse-still in the back corner of the kitchen, I felt brief glimmers of pleasure as I began to appreciate just how helpful the new cupboards and drawers would be.

This was one last time for me to see so many of the skills and tools of a builder in action. On this afternoon there was a virtuoso performance at fast-motion advance speed. Four different electrical saws, an electric plane, nail guns, chisel, and router were in use. Paul and David were flying through boxes searching for different nails and screws, just the right ones, flinging bits in and out of the electric screwdriver, driving the screws in with force backed with the assurance of years of practice.

Then it was entirely dark. Outside the open door, the October woods were dripping from the soft rain. At five David was sent home. Before he left we stood on the porch together, knowing there were no words to thank him for his kindness and help. Then, in a warm, affectionate moment by the car I urged, "You'll come round for coffee sometimes, won't you?" and he gave me his beautiful smile and said, "Of course."

Back inside, I wandered downstairs to a basement that, with its uncovered rafters, felt vast and cave-like. The lights we'd had installed here were throwing good light on a dark night. I picked up wood scraps from the floor. Each different piece had a slightly different smell. The pine and the cedar were especially evocative. In spite of Barry's compulsive sweeping there were fresh piles of fluffy sawdust everywhere.

At six o'clock Paul called me upstairs to look at the finial squares he was cutting for the post ends of the stair rail. "Too big?"

"Fine," I told him, meaning it. Even at this late hour, he took a minute to router the edges, to give them a little distinction. There. That was it. There was a flurry of intensely efficient clean up in which Paul's tools were swept up. And then, incredibly, we were standing together on the front porch. Done and done well. I gave him the album of pictures I had made, recording the process from the first marking out of the lot to the finished structure. We shared the firmest of handshakes and Paul invited us to call him if we had a problem. And then we watched the red truck roll out of the driveway for the last time.

At six-thirty, in silence, we gathered our own things and drove home over roads slick with the wind-driven leaves that were flying down, dodging many frogs who were unwisely crossing on the wet night. I had only the dimmest intimation of a future in our sound, beautiful house.

XI

Leaving Day

A cold rain was falling when, promptly at eight, the large white moving truck rattled up the narrow driveway that led to the supervisor's house. It swung to a halt, almost touching our front door. With a bang the back panel was raised, revealing a cavernous interior. A ramp was slammed down, bridging the distance from truck to door. Quickly, I shut the three shocked cats and anxious Molly in the bathroom, safely out of the confusion of stripping a home. At last, this was leaving day, but I could not, must not think of that.

Inside our house, the moving company owner's eyes darted, mentally maneuvering our contents through narrow doors and down tricky stairs to cram it into the truck's maw. And then the running began. All day the five young men ran as if something about speed hurtled them beyond pain and exhaustion.

"The pictures still on the walls, sir. What do you want us to do with them?" one of the men asked Barry. In the end, we simply had not been able to find time to wrap these securely in preparation for the move. "We'll have to come back for them," Barry told him. Without a word, thoughtfully, carefully, the man fetched proper boxes and tape and within an hour had them all safely crated and loaded into the truck.

Squeezed against a wall, I watched as the men swung chests onto their backs, expertly swishing straps to help themselves. When they hefted my treasured large, old piano onto a dolly and creaked it through the music room, the living room, the sunporch and out to the ramp I could no longer bear to look. As the running feet clattered back and forth through the echoing rooms, the very stuff of my life was being dismantled.

No time. No time for coffee, no time for lunch. There was an uncharacteristic shocked silence from the three cats and Molly, who were still shut in the bathroom. By early afternoon Barry was driving off, accompanying the swaying truck to guide it on its first of two trips across the narrow back roads to our new place.

Now, as I checked the progress, my footfalls clattered in the nearly empty house. Upstairs on the floor lay the remains of a child's rumpled crayon picture. I picked it up, folded it carefully and shoved it in my jeans pocket. After months of work, for now there was nothing more for me to do.

Barry was back from the first trip, and I took strength from his presence. He whispered to me in amusement, "When we got over to the other place, one of the men said 'Jesus. I thought where you did live was lonely and God-forsaken, but now you've moved to the ass-end of the world.'"

It was time. The movers were slamming the truck doors, and latching them shut, ready for their second and last trip. Barry would follow behind me but now I must load the limp cats into their carrying boxes and shepherd the trembling Molly (I was trembling myself) into the car, which I had already stuffed with a jungle of houseplants.

And so we closed the door and turned out the lights on a house that for thirty years had been full of love.

XII

Circling Home

So now it was time to learn to live in our new home. Over the long months of planning and building, we used to try to guess so many things. Now, at last we knew that the light of day travels within our house just as we hoped it would, coming first to our south-facing bedroom, with western light leaving our dining room. And this was important. Indeed, as winter approached, we were cheered to find the low sun flooding in better than Barry's best guess. What was more, the wished-for windows at each end of the central hall drew us ever outwards. Even Barry admitted that now that he was living with them, they pleased him.

All the while we worked at unpacking boxes and stowing their contents we were learning to live with the rise and fall of light. When we rose at night, sleepless with the strangeness of it all, we held each other and watched the moon and the blazing stars travel as we never could before in our previous, narrow-windowed homes. The first time I set up my big yellow gripstand bowl to make bread on the kitchen's peninsula counter, I found that I had a fine view of the last of the brilliant autumn in three different directions from where I stood.

Unfailingly, the superb views out our carefully planned windows lifted our hearts. And, surprisingly, we had need of this. Here we were at last, living in comfort in a sturdy, well-built home. The airy kitchen, with its many drawers and cupboards, had every convenience I could wish for. The compact living room we had created around our central crimson Kilim rug turned out to be a triumph of design. Providing an amazing combination of shelter and openness, it could have been used as an example of Alexander's concept of *architectural compression*, where many aspects were successfully combined in one space.

But, after thirty years of living intensely in one house, not surprisingly, finding new rhythms disoriented us at first. Delicately we danced around each other in the frustrating clutter of moving boxes. Not having our tools available and organized struck raw nerves. Because we were coping with the double losses of Barry's job and our former home, our frequent failures to find common things grated more than they otherwise might have. Discovering simple things, like rulers and the large Maine bell that hangs outside our front door, took on an absurd importance.

Clumsily, we began to establish new routines that would work for us. Zen philosophy teaches constant mindfulness. But, as we thought through every small step of each daily process in a space where everything was unfamiliar, we found that too much awareness was exhausting.

During this time of adjustment, perhaps it was not surprising that I felt I had lost my centre. French philosopher Gaston Bachelard claimed that one of the benefits of a suitable house was that it allows one to dream in peace. After the long process of building and moving, this was what I hungered for. Unfortunately, after I lovingly arranged my books in the tall birch bookcases in my excellent, pink-walled writing room, when I sat down to my desk I discovered that I could not work. Unable to slip into reverie, for all of that winter I felt frozen.

A metamorphosis takes time. While we waited to feel at home enough to be ourselves, we took pleasure in the dailiness of tasks, such as splitting and fetching wood from the long woodpile we stacked. Laying and tending our fires steadied us, and we delighted in the rich warmth cast by our woodstove, and were steadied by its everchanging, dancing flames.

Slowly, slowly, we set up the other inspirational parts of my life in our basement. Thanks to our builders' hard work there, we had been able to bring over everything that was important to me. And then, a few weeks after our move, Morgan and Rick came for a weekend and gave us the precious gift of laying flooring there for us. With the cement covered and cushioned with *red oak* laminate, these downstairs rooms became homelike.

In the central downstairs room we set up our library, lining the walls with shelves. But as I placed our books roughly, to be organized later, I couldn't help wondering how long it would take before I could sleep-walk to lay my hands on an essential volume with ease.

In the studio room, with its many windows and patio doors, there was space to set up my piano as well as the two floor looms, one large and one small, their accompanying floor-to-ceiling shelves of bright-coloured yarns, and even the expansive oak work table that had followed us through all our years together.

All winter, though, as I waited to become used to our new home, I continued to feel vulnerable. It seemed that I would have to learn all over again both to live in the moment and to live simply with what is. Meanwhile, nightmares crowded in. Remembering the ice storm that had toppled so many trees at the park, in my dark moments I feared for the fine large maples, beeches, oaks, and cedars that we loved at Singing Meadow.

Throughout the long process of preparing to leave the park, we had been heartened by the kindness of so many. And, in our new neighbourhood, we were touched to find that the help continued once we moved in. One late autumn afternoon, Bob Stewart drove up on his big tractor. "You'll be wanting a vegetable garden, I suppose. Where would you like me to plough?" Quite wonderfully, by the time the sun had set we looked out on a large rectangle of turned land, a promise for a new start the next year. Next spring, our dear, very old friend Bill MacLean appeared with one of the John Deere tractors he lovingly restored for a hobby, and which he had driven across the back-country roads. "I was thinking you'd want your garden worked up a bit." Both men understood that a house without a vegetable garden was not a home. We could not live here without the generosity of neighbours.

ABIDING: Over my long process of orientation, my constant joy was the land. That first winter, a ghostly owl haunted our valley, often roosting on an elm that overhangs the road near our new home. Rare to eastern Ontario, this Great Grey had fled south from a scarcity in her arctic territory to search for more available food. Almost all huge feathered eyes, the immense, assured presence seemingly stood by us, letting us approach nearly within touching range to watch the swivel of her remarkable head. Then, with the coming of March, she drifted back north to her traditional hunting grounds, leaving us stronger than when she had first appeared.

On a day when large flakes of sugar snow were flying down, I stood watching the plump, brown tree sparrows flitting through a tangle of grape vines. I listened to the clamour of approaching blue jays, hurrying across the valley to our now familiar feeders. Newly returned wild geese rose up from the still half-frozen water meadow, their calls once again echoing from the hills that hold us all. Slowly, clumsily, I knew that I was making my way towards wholeness. I had come here to learn to continue in deepest kinship with the land. And in its own way and time, Singing Meadow was gathering me, weaving me into its whole.

What started me thinking that day was a meeting with our old friend, Bob Prevost, who was newly well after a long struggle with cancer. Naturally, given that it was March, the talk turned to syrup making. "When I was sickest last year," he told me, "my brother took me out to our sugar bush. I couldn't help any, of course, but I just needed to be there. You know what I mean? I even slept over on those cold, spring nights." After that, he asked how we were fitting in with our new home and was pleased that we had found the land we needed. For Bob and me, as it was for Thoreau, our real life was outside. "How could you go to sleep not hearing the whip-poor-will?" he asked. "That was what got me well again."

Now I was walking slowly down to the water meadow, hearing the strange, quarrelsome-sounding talk of herons beginning another season here. I was teaching myself how to be aware every moment of every step so I could keep walking longer on this rough land. With any luck, this beloved place would be my last home. And, after the unignorable message of recent fierce summers, I was here to bear witness, to stand with the great maples, beeches, and oaks through whatever might come, to accompany with whatever grace I could for as long as I could sustain it. Living here, this was who I wanted to be — an old woman vanishing into the light.

Soon, it would be time to go indoors again to our welcoming home. But only for a while. Sometimes, though, I had a new dream. No longer here in body, I was floating, reduced purely to tenderness, brooding the land with my great love.

Barry

After ten joyous years at Singing Meadow, our sky fell in. Last summer we were shocked to learn that Barry had metastasized cancer. Most cruelly, his only apparent symptom was a tumour pressing on his upper spine, which swiftly lead to a creeping paralysis, much like that experienced by ALS sufferers.

Hastily our family was challenged to put together a plan which included having Barry home from hospital for November and December. Fumbling to work with our diminished life, it seemed that the only remaining thing we knew for sure was that only love could save us.

As more and more of him was taken away, Barry never failed in courage, reaching out whenever he could. Through this brief, agonizing journey, we felt utterly surrounded by love from family, friends, neighbours, the people of Westport, the superb big support team that came together to help make home care possible, and eventually, for his last week in Kingston General, the magnificent doctors, residents and nurses there.

When he contracted pneumonia, with cancer-compromised lungs and extensive paralysis, his big heart simply couldn't defeat it. After a tough week, he slipped away easily into a stormy night. He begged me not to leave him, and it comforts me to say that I never did.

Since then I have been comforted by the messages from many who tell me that Barry's life mattered, that he made a difference in their lives and that he will not be forgotten. "I can't tell you how sorry I am for all of us — we've lost a great human being." Most of all I am heartened by the inspiration of our profound love for each other, which is everywhere here at Singing Meadow.

My task now, in the midst of unspeakable grief, my gift to my beloved life partner, is to learn to turn away from the shadows.

While I am still given the astonishing gift of life I want to face into the sun. Barry, and the ravens, and the feathery pine trees would expect no less of me.

Afterword

... which is included here because Barry and I always prefer books in which a little is revealed of what happened next.

THE VILLAGE: Since we moved to Singing Meadow, as well as Barry, inevitably we lost some of those who loved Foley Mountain and knew how important it was, including long-time reeve, Bill Thake, pharmacist Brenda Palmer, and friend Bob Prevost. However, many newcomers have embraced the spirit of our special community and have brought new strengths to it.

FOLEY MOUNTAIN: After dark political years while Barry was Area Supervisor, vision and diligent work by the Rideau Valley Conservation Authority and the Friends of Foley Mountain have protected the park's future and added improvements, such as the new log education centre in the student campground. The education program has been strengthened and broadened by grants that encourage more classes to experience nature first-hand. These days, the park has a new supervisor, our friend Rebecca Whitman, who lives with her husband, Jeff, and two little boys in the park house. (And yes, I am happy to say that the Whitmans have carried on with our vegetable garden.) Following on what Barry began long ago, Rebecca has added her own style and improvements. Meanwhile, I feel fortunate to be able to continue to walk the trails at the park.

SINGING MEADOW: Barry and I never took our great fortune in living here for granted. We took joy in walking here after our move with our family, enjoying doing pond studies both here and at Foley Mountain with another generation, our dear grandchildren Liam and Natalie.

I have lived here long enough now to see the trees we planted wave over our heads. In fact, last summer the song sparrow raised two broods in a grassy nest in one of our spruces. On winter nights, they shelter the small birds who flock to our feeders.

Our own vegetable garden has fed us abundantly, while the messy but beloved flower gardens have fed our souls. As do the foxes, skunks, bear, deer, and deliciously absurd wild turkeys who pass us on their way to and from the valley.

Over time, we also experienced the building of a new, affectionate community among our neighbours. Of a summer's day, you might find some of us out in the meadow counting wildflowers, or by evening, clustered on a deck watching flying squirrels.

Acknowledgements

In memory of two dear friends who gave us joy and who live on in our hearts, **David Pritchard** *and* **Umberto D'Antini.**

Rena Upitis, of Wintergreen Studios, who, with her vision and dedication, is an inspiration to us all. Rena truly understood what was in my heart and most needed saying and gave me the opportunity to do so.

Sara Beck, honorary daughter and the warmest of editors.

Our sons, Morgan and Jeremy, and their spouses, Rick and Karen, as well as our grandchildren, Liam and Natalie, for their generous encouragement, always.

My sister, Lisa Moses, and my niece, Megan Trickett, and her family, have heartened me along the way.

The best of neighbours, with special mention to Bob Stewart, Paul, Marilyn, and Scott Clasby, and Dr. Steve Moore.

Our friends, who believed in us, Joy and Graham Fielder.

Our builders, Paul Musselman and David Pollard, and their crew, who worked hard to make our dreams a reality.

Terry Martin, his son Justin, brother Eddie, and nephew Allan. Although Terry is gone now, his caring work continues. Terry, we often think you are still watching out for us.

The people of Westport, a community that just keeps getting better.

Bibliography

... a brief sampling of books that inspired me on my search.

Alexander, Christopher (1977). *A pattern language.* Berkeley: Center for Environmental Structure.

Bachelard, Gaston (1969). *The poetics of space.* Boston: Beacon.

Bachelard, Gaston (1971). *The poetics of reverie.* Boston: Beacon.

Beresford-Kroeger, Diana (2003). *Arboretum America: A philosophy of the forest.* Michigan: The University of Michigan Press.

Beresford-Kroeger, Diana (2013). *The sweetness of a simple life: Tips for healthier, happier and kinder living, gleaned from the wisdom and science of nature.* Canada: Random House Canada.

Carroll, David M. (1999). *Swampwalker's journal.* Boston: Houghton Mifflin.

Davidson, Laura Lee (1924). *Isles of Eden.* New York: Minton, Balch & Company.

Davidson, Laura Lee (1924). A *winter of content.* New York: The Abingdon Press.

de Kiriline Lawrence, Louise (1968). *The lovely and the wild.* NY: McGraw-Hill.

Hoover, Helen (1965). *The long-shadowed forest.* London: Souvenir.

Hoover, Helen (1973). *The years of the forest.* NY: Knopf.

Jones, Lloyd Bernard (2002). *Living by the chase: The native people of Crow and Bobs Lakes.* Belleville, ON: Epic Press.

Jones, Lloyd Bernard (2003). *The damned lakes: An environmental history of Crow and Bobs Lakes* (3rd ed.). Belleville, ON: Epic Press.

Kidder, Tracy (1999). *House.* New York: Houghton Mifflin Mariner Books.

Leslie, Clare Walker (1984). *The art of field sketching.* New Jersey: Prentice-Hall Inc.

Leslie, Clare Walker, and Roth, Charles E. (1998). *Nature journaling: Learning to observe and connect with the world around you.* VT: Storey Books.

Macy, Joanna (1991). *World as lover, world as self.* Berkeley, CA: Parallax Press.

McQuay, Peri Phillips (1995). *The view from Foley Mountain.* Toronto, ON: Natural Heritage.

McQuay, Peri Phillips (2001). *A wing in the door.* Minneapolis, MN: Milkweed Editions.

Peden, Rachel (2009). *Rural free: A farmwife's almanac of country living.* Indiana: Indiana University Press.

Pollan, Michael (2008). *A Place of my own: The architecture of daydreams.* NY: Bantam Doubleday Dell Publishing Group, Inc.

Susanka, Sara (1998). *The not so big house.* CT: Taunton Press.

Susanka, Sara (2001). *Creating the not so big house.* CT: Taunton.

Teale, Edwin Way (1974). *A naturalist buys an old farm.* NY: Dodd Mead.

Theberg, John, and Theberg, Mary (2011). *The ptarmigan's dilemma: An ecological exploration into the mysteries of life.* Toronto, ON: McClelland & Stewart.

Ureneck, Lou (2011). *Cabin: Two brothers, a dream, and five acres in Maine.* New York: Penguin Books.

Wiggins, Glenn B. (2009). *Biological notes on an old farm: Exploring common things in the kingdoms of life.* Toronto, ON: Royal Ontario Museum.

Wintergreen Studios Press is an independent literary press. It is affiliated with the not-for-profit educational retreat centre, Wintergreen Studios, and supports the work of Wintergreen Studios by publishing works related to education, the arts, and the environment.

www.wintergreenstudios.com

69878433R00114

Made in the USA
Columbia, SC
30 April 2017